The Savvy Horsey Mum:

How To Juggle Kids & Horses Successfully!

(And why it's important to continue to pursue your horsey passions...)

Sarah Walkerden

Written & Published By:

Sarah Walkerden
Founder of the Horsey Mums Collective &
Owner/Manager of One Stop Horse Shop

Horsey Mums Collective
www.horseymumscollective.com
One Stop Horse Shop
www.onestophorse.com.au

© 2018 Sarah Walkerden

(First Edition October 2018)

Disclaimer:
The author and associated entities shall have neither liability nor responsibility to any person or entity with respect to any loss or damage caused or alleged to be caused directly or indirectly by the information contained within this book. Whilst this book is as accurate as possible, there may be errors, omissions or inaccuracies. All information and suggestions are intended to be of general in nature, and readers should seek professional support in relation to their own specific circumstances.

ISBN: 978-0-6484431-0-0 (Kindle)
ISBN: 978-0-6484431-1-7 (PDF / EBook)
ISBN: 978-0-6484431-2-4 (Paperback)
ISBN: 978-0-6484431-3-1 (Amazon Paperback)

Dedication

I dedicate this book to my amazing husband (and best friend) Toby and my beautiful children - Oliver & Sophie.

And to all my amazing fellow 'horsey mums' out there...
.
Stay strong and never give up on your dreams!

CONTENTS

INTRODUCTION
Why am I writing this book?

Quite simply, I want to inspire all those amazing 'horsey' mums out there to keep riding. To keep their horses, to hold on to their horsey dreams and goals, and to never give up on their passion.

The 'dream' might look different, for each individual mum. For some, it might simply be riding at a trail ride centre once a month. For others, it might be keeping their own horse (or many!) with the goal of riding several times a week – and even aiming for competitive pursuits.

It doesn't matter what does it for you. It doesn't matter how humble or how lofty your dreams and goals are.

What's important is that you don't lose YOU!

For me, horses are a part of WHO I AM. They aren't a mere recreational pursuit. They aren't JUST an animal or a pet. And they certainly AREN'T NEGOTIABLE. I CANNOT and WILL NOT survive the daily grind of 'life' without a horse (and preferably several!).

Horses are my freedom. They allow me to escape the craziness of 'reality' and just be in the moment. When I am with my horses, no one and nothing else exists. Time does not exist. For someone like me, who is a bit of a work-a-holic, a 'stress-head', and who often suffers from anxiety, horses bring me back down to earth. They allow my stress to dissolve, and my head and body to calm down, and stop racing. Horses are the only thing that can do that for me.

I don't know about you, but I am a fiercely independent kind of woman. Learning to share my life with my (also fiercely independent) husband was difficult enough. But add a baby (and subsequent children) to that mix, and all of a sudden, your life is not yours. It really is incredible how one little tiny screaming human, can render you completely useless.

Where once you could choose what you did, where you went, what time things occurred etc, with a new baby, you suddenly can't even go to the toilet when you need to, let alone shower, or grab a bite to eat. And don't even get me started on the lack of sleep!

But the thing that hit me hardest, was the emotional toll. I will never forget the instant fear that took hold of me, once my first child was born. The earthshaking knowledge, that this tiny creature, was in my care and I was solely responsible for his survival. And the sheer terror of wondering how on earth I was going to keep him safe.

Because I knew if anything happened to him – well life just wouldn't be anything.

Motherhood changes you – the instant that child comes out of your amazing body. You are never the same person, ever again. And no matter what your well-meaning husband might say or believe – they (men) generally get to keep on living. Our lives, as a mum however, tends to stop – at least in some way.

To add to this confusing and overwhelming mix of responsibility and emotions, society adds its' own beliefs and perceptions on to you, which tend to weigh down heavily on to our already exhausted shoulders.

Other people in your life, whether they are friends, family or strangers, and no matter how well meaning, or how un-realistic they might be – they all have their expectations on how you, as a mother, should behave, how to conduct your life, and how to raise your child.

The whole system can be really unfair.

After all, a mother tends to put herself under more than enough pressure, without any outside assistance. We constantly feel like we are failing our children. That we aren't even 'good enough'.

That our child's inability to sleep, reluctance to eat, or poor behaviour, or any number of issues, is all our fault! So why must others insist on judging us so harshly – as we are usually our own toughest and most unfair critic anyway.

Sarah Walkerden

Trouble is – often these well-meaning people in our lives don't even realise that they are doing it!

So it's not unusual, even in todays modern, and somewhat more equal world, that us mums give up on our passions. We put ourselves, our lives, and our hopes and dreams on hold, in an effort to be the best mum we can be.

And in some cases, maybe this is the best option. No one can tell you what is going to work in your particular circumstances. And sometimes a short break from other pursuits, particularly immediately after a baby arrives, might indeed be necessary. But giving up on your hobbies, your interests and your passions entirely, will not serve you well.

Because giving up on who you are – will only lead to your unhappiness. And if a mother is unhappy, well, her family and kids will undoubtedly suffer. Because all of us mums would know – an unhappy mum rubs off and can often create a very unhappy family.

Therefore, to maintain our own energy levels, we all need a break from time to time. And time to just be 'us'.

So I am here to tell you, that life doesn't have to stop (or at least not for too long!). I am here to tell you, that you really can – and SHOULD – have it all. And yes – you can indeed keep your horse!

It IS POSSIBLE to have babies and kids, whilst retaining at least some, or if not all, of your chosen and much-loved horsey pursuits.

And I am here to tell you how.

Now, if you have stumbled across this book, and don't own or ride horses, or don't have any involvement in horses whatsoever, please don't think this book cannot help you. Because yes, whilst we are focussing on the specific logistics and benefits of staying involved with horses, you can replace the 'horse' with any other passions, interests or goals that you have. It really is a case of 'mothers uniting'. We are still people and we are still individuals, even after becoming a mum.

My intention however is certainly not to underestimate or under-value the importance of your children. No matter what – we love them and will always put their wellbeing first. It is simply to encourage you to maintain a healthy balance in life – in order for you to feel as if you are still important too.

And for any of the horsey husbands or partners out there – you can (and should!) read this too. If it gives you even the tiniest bit of understanding, when it comes to your beloved horse obsessed partner, and why horses are important to them – then my job will be done.

Horses are healthy. I know they are expensive, and time consuming, and they might seem annoying.

But if they make your partner happy and help her retain her sanity – then it will make your lives happier and more successful. It is totally worth your while to muster up as much support for her endeavours, as you can possibly manage. Trust me on that one.

And with no further ado, let's get into it.

CHAPTER 1:
Why Riding is Healthy AND Important (Before & After Kids)

I firmly believe that horse riding is hugely beneficial, whether it be purely as a hobby or recreational pursuit, or as a competitive sport. For us women, who have been lucky enough to have been hit with the 'horse bug' it clearly has both physical and mental/emotional benefits.

Let's focus on the physical benefits of horse riding to start with. Whilst much of this might appear obvious, let's cover this anyway – particularly for any of those non-horsey husbands out there (or mother-in-laws!).

Horse riding gets you outside in the fresh air. Simply walking to the paddock, and then across a paddock to catch your horse, gets you active. And then you need to walk them back out of that paddock, to an area to tie them up. You then proceed to brush them thoroughly and vigorously, fetch your gear out of the tack room (or possibly out of your car if you agist), saddle up, ride, un-tack, put gear away, make up horse feed, give said horsey feed, and then put your horse back in to the paddock he came from (as an example of one routine that might occur).

All of this clearly takes a reasonable amount of physical effort. Any activity that encourages such physical effort, keeps you fitter, healthier and stronger.

Many 'non-horsey' folk just love to suggest that horse riding itself, requires little effort from the rider. That the horse 'does all the work'. Familiar story?

This is (as most horsey mums would know) a GREAT BIG MYTH (and I do hope those horsey partners out there are listening to this).

Because any horse rider, of any standard, or any discipline knows, that riding takes one hell of an effort – particularly to get it 'right'. We are not just sitting up there, like a sack of potatoes.

Our bodies do a lot of work in order to get the best out of our horses. You need a certain level of energy and fitness to ride for any length or time, and to ride well. But not only that, you need a lot of muscle strength and flexibility. Our riding muscles work ridiculously hard – making them ridiculously strong.

And it is often this strength, which becomes a great bonus when it comes to pregnancy, child birth and postnatal recovery. A fit, strong, active and healthy mother will always cope with the demands of pregnancy and birth better, then one that has a more sedentary lifestyle. And this is something that has been well proven, and most doctors will recommend maintaining an active lifestyle. So, bear in mind, that fit and strong women, always cope better.

Do the nature of wrangling a 500kg wild animal(!) – and having to lift and carry large heavy saddles, horse gear, bags of horse feed, bales of hay – this also has huge benefits to our physical strength and muscle tone! No gym membership required!

In a nutshell – 'Horsey Women' are damn tough and strong!

The mental and emotional side to riding however, is also equally (and if not more so) important. Pre AND Post-Natal Depression is becoming more and more common. Mothers (or mothers to be) quite often struggle with all the demands placed upon them. And in this litigation focussed modern world, doctors tend to be extra cautious. And whilst I would never ever recommend going against your doctors advice, please be aware that their cautious nature will generally tend to lead them towards recommending that mothers are cautious about horses. And caution is fine, so long as it doesn't stop you from living.

You can never really put yourself in a bubble to protect yourself, and your little ones, from every single danger in life. Whilst yes, you do need to modify your routines and procedures whilst pregnant and post-birth to minimise potential risk as much as possible, I am here to encourage you to not stop living. Ever!

If your happiness comes from hanging out with your horses – then don't stop. Modify what you do and how you do it, but never ever stop.

Whether you choose to ride during pregnancy or not, is up to your personal circumstances and beliefs to decide, but certainly don't avoid your horses all together, unless you must be confined to a bed.

Because quite frankly, a miserable mother, is of no use to anyone.

If you do find yourself with pregnancy or after-birth complications, be kind to yourself. Delegate horse care tasks where you can, and get hubby, or the owner of the agistment property, or anyone you can – to take some photos of your beloved beasts.

Spend the time daydreaming about horses. Know that this is only temporary – that things will get better, and your horses will still be there when you are fit and able once again.

The Ever-So-Slight Downside

Whilst horses are indeed hugely beneficial, there is also a slight downside to all of this that I've found affected me, and the horsey mums around me, with the birth of their children.

Due to the fact that us 'Horsey Mums' gain a lot of mental and emotional 'toughness' from dealing with horses (as horses need you to be cool, calm & confident), whilst this is absolutely a great advantage to have – it can also be a bit of a disadvantage.

When we are so used to being so capable, independent and strong – it can come as quite a shock to us when one tiny little human baby can bring our lives to such a screaming halt – and make us feel quite helpless.

This is something I really struggled with, as I was so used to my freedom and being able to do so much. You soon discover however that newborn babies take every single ounce of energy, patience and resilience that you can possibly muster. And that where once you were galloping freely outside with the horses, fixing fences and wrangling those giant but beautiful beasts of yours – the frustration of being forced to pace endlessly around the house with a screaming baby – or getting stuck sitting on the couch for hours on end, each and every day, with a child sleeping on top of you (because they won't sleep otherwise!) – is intense!

I tell you this so you can be slightly better prepared for it than I was and therefore my hope is that you may be able to cope better with this frustration and impatience.

All I can say – if you struggle with this like I did – know it does get better as your kids get older. Babies grow and become more independent. And some level of freedom can be yours once again. You've just got to wait it out and survive!

On the flip side though, this mental and emotional strength we have can indeed help us to cope with the battles of child raising that little bit better. My husband is very fond of saying that you can basically train children in the same way as horses! Both require consistency, patience, and firm but fair boundaries!

If All Else Fails – Go Cuddle The Horse!

The best thing ever about being a 'Horsey Mum' is the fact that you have your very own personal therapist, on tap, out in the paddock whenever you need him/her.

Your children WILL drive you to the brink of insanity. But in that moment, where you finally get five minutes, to race outside to the paddock and cuddle your horse – you can escape.

Nothing is quite as soothing as being able to share your troubles with your horse, whilst you bury your face into his mane, have him snuffling his sweet horsey breath down the back of your neck – or tickling your face with his whiskers. It's in those moments that you find peace.

And you'll be able to return to your family calmer and happier.

It's magic!

CHAPTER 2:
Preparing For Kids & Setting Realistic Expectations

The Joys of Pregnancy(!)

There are lots of things you can do to make looking after your horses easier, before kids arrive on the scene. But it is also important to realise upfront, that life WILL change, and your ability to manage your horses and ride – will also change.

One cannot expect life to continue as normal, when battling pregnancy, child birth and new babies. And a temporary period of 'horsey hiatus' will likely ensue. How long that break might last, will come down to individual circumstances. Yet if you put plans in place beforehand and do your best to remain patient – please do know that things WILL get easier.

So, what can you do to make looking after your horses easier?

The answer is to SIMPLIFY! Because it is such a huge topic, I have devoted the entire next chapter to ways in which you can simplify your horse care and management, as much as possible.

But let's talk EXPECTATIONS first as making sure we are realistic about what's to come will help us to manage better.

Often us 'Super Women' plan and expect to become 'Super Mums' who can handle having babies, and keep riding, without a care in the world. It's gonna be easy right? Ride throughout your pregnancy, back on the horse a few weeks after birth, park your kid in a stroller beside the arena – and hey presto – easy peasy mothering and horsing.

Ummm, maybe this might be the case, for a few lucky mums, particularly the more competitive and professional active riders, who have straightforward placid children and plenty of support - they MIGHT be able to achieve this. And if this is you – then I take my hat off to you and admire you incredibly.

However! For the rest of us, things might not always go that smoothly. It really isn't until you fall pregnant, and get to around the 6 week mark, that the realities of how hard pregnancy can be, will actually hit. It was around 5 – 6 weeks, in both my pregnancies, that the joy of morning sickness hit me. And no, it wasn't mild. It was 24/7 queasiness, with dry reaching, sheer exhaustion, not being able to eat and barely able to function, type morning sickness.

At the time, I was working in corporate jobs, in quiet formal offices. I did my best to concentrate at my desk on work, and then quietly slip away to the toilets when the nausea got too much (across the other side of the floor), to hurl (as quietly and professionally as possible haha), and then did my best to stumble dizzily back through the office, and slump into my chair, hoping to hell I could sit there for another 5 minutes without losing my stomach on the floor!

There were some days I couldn't get out of bed – and was forced to call in sick. At weekends, when I would have liked to have been out with my horses, I lay on the couch – quietly dying (or so it felt at the time!).

This is how I spent the first four to five months of both my pregnancies. It was sheer hell! All whilst my chirpy husband happily galloped around the property doing 'normal' stuff, such as fixing fences and gardening – with the occasional – 'Can I get you anything, dear' when he popped his head in the door.

It was frustrating!

If you are lucky enough to not experience morning sickness to this degree, then I envy you. But I also know, that other women experience morning sickness even worse than I did. So it's wise to plan for this time – and be aware of this stage, before it happens (where possible). After all, the horses will still need feeding – somehow!

If the morning sickness subsides a little at some point during your pregnancy, for me at around four to five months it was a little (and I mean a LITTLE) easier – you then get to the stage where your growing belly starts getting in the way – and pregnancy starts to really wear you out. Growing a baby puts an incredible toll on your body, and the exhaustion is really quite something.

I was also really lucky to receive the gift of 'stretching-pains'. By this I mean as my tummy grew – my muscles through my back, ribs and down my sides, struggled to catch up. I have always had a bad back anyway and have always been super slim (don't hate me!), so my body struggled a little under the strain. And I guess this is where being on the healthy, fit and strong end of the spectrum may put you at a slight disadvantage.

At times, particularly later in pregnancy, I could barely walk through the pain. With my belly so heavy and taking over my entire body, it meant my rib cage was being forced to expand outwards, and I could literally feel the muscles in my sides (between my ribs and hips) being torn and stretched with every step I took. The only thing that saved me, whilst running around in the city doing my corporate job, was wearing a pregnancy tummy support and seeing an Osteo. Osteopaths are amazing people – and mine certainly relived a hell of a lot of pain. It seriously helped my body cope with the strain of pregnancy and made life somewhat more comfortable.

But the real point of these stories, is to let you know that looking after your horses during this time, can be really tricky. And whether you intend to ride or not, it can get quite impossible, or at the very least incredibly uncomfortable, as your pregnancy progresses.

So, the key is to set realistic expectations! Ensure you enlist the support of your husband, or family, or friends, or pay someone to help you feed horses, if it's needed.

I personally did not ride much at all whilst pregnant. Early on, the morning sickness was so intense, that I think I managed to ride once in the first 12 weeks, and that was it. After that, exhaustion and an uncomfortable body prevented it.

I also did really worry about the chance of accidents – as I've never been an overly confident rider and my horses were never completely bombproof. The general medical advice on this is within the first 12 weeks of pregnancy riding is relatively low risk as baby is small and well protected within your tummy. After that 12 week mark when you start to grow a visible tummy, the risk increases as your baby is more exposed.

I personally decided that I just didn't want to risk any of my babies. But the risk is something that you must weigh up as an individual – and in consultation with your partner and medical professionals.

If you do want to ride, it's wise to stick to a quieter horse, and make sure you have someone else around, just in case.

But if you plan to ride, and then don't end up being able to – don't despair or be too hard on yourself. Pregnancies are unpredictable. No matter how much you plan, things never seem to go according to that plan. And a few months break for your horse, isn't going to hurt him/her.

A Note On Feeding Safety

I feel it's wise to note here the safety aspects of actually being able to feed your horse/s – without too much fuss.

Often horses get rather excited the moment their feed buckets appear or when someone approaches their paddock. Some horses allow this excitement and impatience for their feed to get the better of them and will become quite boisterous (or even aggressive) towards you or anyone else carrying the buckets.

If you have multiple horses kept together, they will quite often 'argue' amongst themselves (in the form of putting their ears back, biting and kicking) – which can get dangerous if you end up in the firing line.

Before babies arrive on the scene, please ensure your horses are SAFE and respectful of you during feeding time.

Each of your horses should know that he/she MUST BE POLITE when you step anywhere near their paddock (regardless of the presence of a feed bucket!).

They should wait patiently, or at least follow you nicely (without any pushing) and wait for you to place their buckets down and for you to give them permission to start eating – BEFORE they dive their head in(!).

This is really crucial to keep yourself safe, your 'bump' safe whilst you are pregnant, and anyone else, who needs to feed them in your absence, SAFE.

If you have a particularly feed aggressive horse – a lunge whip or training stick can be a very handy implement to have. Whilst I would never recommend beating or hitting a horse with anything – a quick flick of a lunge whip towards their hindquarters, or a firm 'thwack' of a rope or stick on the ground to startle them – will help keep you safe – and teach them that bad behaviour is unacceptable.

But if you struggle with this – please call in some professional help.

This is something you'd want to sort out anyway (regardless of pregnancy and babies) – but if you think there might be issues that could escalate with an inexperienced handler (i.e. your husband or mum!), or if they crop up at any stage in your pre-baby planning – then it's wise to catch these early and instil the appropriate rules and manners in your horse as quickly as you can.

Newborn Planning

It's also a good idea to plan for the first 3 – 12 months after your new baby arrives. Whilst you might have great intentions of being back in the saddle straight away, this may not always be possible.

Generally, doctors recommend not riding for the first three months to allow your body to heal and recover. This advice is solid – and something you should probably follow (unless you are one of these miraculous, super-fit, super-strong mums, who can get back on the horse after two weeks!).

And then there is the sleep deprivation and lack of energy, when you are dealing with a newborn.

And sure, you may be luckier than I was. Your child might well sleep perfectly, from the get-go. I really hope for your sake that this is true.

However, my babies never did. They spent more time awake, and more time screaming, than they ever did asleep. With both kids, I jumped back on my horse briefly, at around the 12-13 week mark. Both times celebrating and patting myself on the back for being so awesome and capable. And then I didn't manage to ride again, until closer to the 12 month mark. Damn!

The key to retaining your sanity here, is to be patient. You WILL get back to riding, EVENTUALLY! But whilst you are navigating the murky waters of the first 12 months of having your baby, simply aim to find the time, to go out and pat and cuddle your horse, a few times a week.

Beg your husband, enlist your mum, your mother-in-law, your best friend, your next-door neighbour, anyone who wants a 'baby cuddle'. You hand that baby over, any chance you get granted, and RUN TO THE PADDOCK!

Even five minutes a week with your horse, will help to keep your sanity in check.

CHAPTER 3:
Simplifying Your Horse Care

So here we come to one of the biggest sections of all. How do you manage to look after and feed your horses, whilst you are potentially out of action? It might seem a daunting thing to consider, but rest assured, you can find ways of making your horse feeding routines easier and less time consuming, and possibly outsource some basic aspects of daily horse care.

The first question you need to ask yourself is: How many horses do I have VS How many horses do I actually NEED?

So, whilst I am clearly an advocate for holding on to your horses, this is an aspect which deserves a small mention. Many of us have multiple horses. It is quite rare that us horse crazy women have just one single horse(!). If you do just have one horse, then you can skip this section. But if you have more than a couple, please keep reading. And all of this is said in the most loving manner, with the best of intentions.

It might be worthwhile re-evaluating whether there are any horses that might be best being re-homed, or possibly leased out, at least temporarily.

Generally, younger horses or more difficult horses, or those that require more feed, may be more time intensive and costly to keep. If you want to ride, an older, steadier mount is always the best idea, particularly during pregnancy (if you choose to do so) and particularly when you first return to riding after having a child.

If you can manage to cut down on the numbers you need to look after on a daily basis, then it might be worthwhile considering.

If you can't, don't worry – I get it! You love them all, right? Me too! I had four when I fell pregnant with my first child, and there was no way in hell that I would have parted with any of them!

Horsey Living Arrangements

Once you're convinced you have the right number of horses for you(!), it's time to look at their living arrangements.

Does your horse live with you in your own paddocks – or do you agist? These two scenarios are obviously very different ones to consider.

If you have the option, keep your horses at home, even if you don't have riding facilities. If this is an option, it's always going to best to have your horses close to you, to make feeding (and pony cuddling!) easier.

If you do need to agist your horse somewhere else, then you may be able to look at ways of making their care simpler and most cost effective (remember, money can be tight after babies, with less income whilst you aren't working!).

For example, if you agist your horses at an expensive boutique agistment centre, where they are stabled or paddocked in a small paddock, and requiring hand feeding several times a day, then this might be worth looking at changing. Before kids whilst time is your own – such an agistment property, with it's fancy riding facilities, might be perfect! However once you are pregnant and then once baby arrives, as mentioned earlier, things are gonna change! Those fancy riding facilities may not be used quite so often.

Therefore, it might be wise to ask yourself, would your horse be happier and healthier, if for example he was turned out into a large, shared grassy paddock? One that costs $20-$30 per week, rather than $100? One where he can entertain himself, gallop and play with other horsey friends, whilst you are missing in action? One that does not necessarily require as much hard feed or hay?

Location can also be a good aspect to consider. If you manage to get a whole two hours to go play with your horse, baby free, you don't want to waste much of that time, simply travelling. The closer your horse, the easier it is to go see him.

If you do have your horses at home, you might like to look at re-evaluating your paddocks and paddock management too. Look at how you can set things up, for ease of feeding, rotating appropriately to make the grass grow, or throwing multiple horses out together, rather than separating them into tiny areas.

Or you might find separating horses into smaller paddocks easier to manage, particularly if you have a dominant one that dominates the feed!

Figure out what it is that is potentially going to make life easier for you – and get these things organised as early as possible.

Feeding

The number one question here again is, how EASY can you make the feeding process?

Can you look at the feed he is getting, and make it simpler?

I.e.: Cut out the complicated supplements, and 20 different scoops of different feeds.

Can you feed one pre-mixed feed, chaff, either grass or hay, and that's it?

Can you just feed chaff and oats?

Consult an equine nutritionist if you need to. But the trick is to find the simplest regime and the least amount that you can feed, to keep your horse healthy.

My personal preference to keep things easy, is to pick one single 'complete feed' such as a pellet or muesli mix, feed according to the instructions on the bag, and just add chaff.

The way I figure it, is the big feed companies have the equine nutritionists and expertise to balance feed appropriately with the right vitamin &

minerals etc. – which is beyond my (current) skillset (and my time & patience!).

One of my favourite products is HYGAIN ALLROUNDER as a basic pelleted complete feed for many easy-keeping horses in light to medium work, with no major health concerns.

For a younger horse, or one who requires weight gain, I head for HYGAIN TRU BREED, or for an older horse I'd go for HYGAIN TRU CARE.

But this is purely personal preference, and there are plenty of good brands and feeds available, so it pays to do your own research.

And if your horse has any other health concerns (such as laminitis, ulcers, metabolic concerns etc) then you do need to choose the right feed to suit.

(And as a side-note, I have no particular affiliation with Hygain or anyone else.)

Next comes hay – which is clearly required If you have no (or limited) grass. Round bales will most likely be your best friends. I know there is wastage, but if you can throw one out in the paddock to keep the horses happy once a week or so, it's going to be easier than having to feed smaller amounts twice a day (particularly during those early days when bubs can be unpredictably fussy!).

If your horse can survive on hay alone, and no hard feed, then even better for you!

However, if your horse is slightly higher maintenance, and there is nothing you can do to change that, then you will need to enlist help. If you currently visit your horse twice a day to feed, see if you can find someone who can do it for you.

Whether you pay an agistment property, a horse-minding pro, or find a local helpful and enthusiastic horse crazy teenager - see who you can bring in.

Or if you like, leasing your horse/s out can be great too. There are clearly many pitfalls, and you do need to be careful – but if you are out of action for a while, and there is someone around who needs a horse to ride (and can therefore feed it in return), then this could be a great arrangement. Just always insist on a good solid contract and thoroughly check the credentials of anyone who applies before making any decisions.

There are many different things you can do to make your horse-life simpler, easier and less time-consuming. It really does depend on what is going to suit you, your horse and your circumstances and preferences. And its always wise to know that even with the best laid plans, and best intentions, things can go a bit haywire with kids, at any stage.

So finding horsey friends, or people around who can help you, particularly at short notice, is always a useful thing. You just never know when you or your child might be sick and you are left with the panic of having no one around to feed the horses.

ALWAYS HAVE A CONTINGENCY PLAN!

If your horses are on your property, keeping your horses feeding simple, will also assist your husband, or anyone else who needs to help you feed your horses (particularly during the time you spend in hospital with bubs).

Line up your feed bags neatly, write a list of what needs to be fed and when, and pin it above your bags. Keep a good supply of buckets at the ready, with plenty of feed scoops.

This will make things simple for hubby, your non-horsey mum, or in the case of unexpected emergencies, any helpful person who comes to assist, so they can see what your horses need, and then prepare it appropriately and get it to your horses without any headaches.

Being super duper organised is key!

To help you with this process, we have a couple of free downloads that you can simply print off and fill out. You can find them here https://horseymumscollective.com/project/freebies/.

Sarah Walkerden

CHAPTER 4:
After The Birth – Juggling Baby & Horse Care

So your little bundle of (screaming) joy has arrived. Congratulations! Welcome to the scariest and most overwhelming part of your life. Hooray!

You get yourself and baby home from hospital and do your best to settle down. Regardless of whether you birthed naturally, or via caesarean, your body will take time to heal and recover.

And you do need to allow for that process. It will be frustrating, it may well be painful, but please know that it will get better.

In the first three months after having a baby, it is generally recommended by health professionals to not ride horses. But always ask your doctors or midwives as to what is best in your circumstances. You may be strong enough at six weeks if you're really lucky.

I always felt that recovering from childbirth was ridiculously unfair on us poor mothers. Because regardless of how 'easy' or difficult a birth might be, it takes its toll. In many circumstances, you are essentially recovering from major surgery.

Regardless of whether it's your tummy or your lady bits that get ripped apart and sewn back up, it truly sucks!

Yet unlike other surgeries, you don't get time to recover. Because the instant the 'main event' is over, you are responsible for the care of your baby. And even with assistance, you don't get to rest, sleep or recover for long. Add to that the scary and overwhelming cocktail of hormones that sweep through your system – and it can be a recipe for pure hell!

And quite often, no one warns you about any of this.

All I can offer you in those early days, is to try and be patient. Let go of any guilt, and just do what you need to do to keep your baby safe, well and happy (or as happy as can be), and yourself as healthy as possible. Do your best to sleep when the chance arises, eat and drink as healthily and as regularly as possible. Forget housework, forget worrying about your horses too much, just survive it.

Hopefully, before or at least during your pregnancy, you simplified your horses living and feeding requirements as much as possible. Keep it all basic and enlist as much support as you can find.

If you find you are struggling a little too much – please get help. Post Natal Depression is common, and these days there is plenty of help available. Check with your Child and Maternal Health Care Nurse, your GP, or talk to your friends and family. If you get brushed off – ask someone else!

Never be too afraid or embarrassed to talk about how you feel and to ask for extra help!

But despite all of this – do your best to enjoy your baby! For me, the first six months were somewhat torturous with the lack of sleep and lack of freedom.

But it wasn't all doom and gloom! Nothing quite beats that first cute baby smile, or the amazement as you watch your tiny little human learn to roll over, meet milestones, and entertain you with their developing personalities.

These early days also prove just how powerful you, as a woman, and as a person, can really be. We are so much more resilient and often 'super-human' than we might realise with what we can survive and achieve as a mother.

And these days, I figure, if I can survive the baby hell, I can survive just about anything – and so can you!

Sarah Walkerden

CHAPTER 5:
Getting Your Body Back!

When I attended the local 'new mums' support group after the birth of my first child, I remember they had a physiotherapist come in to chat to us about health and fitness. The key thing that stuck in my mind that she told us at that session, was that it takes 12 whole months for your body to recover fully from pregnancy and childbirth. Yes – an entire year! Now admittedly, she stated it in relation to when it might be appropriate to having a second child – but nethertheless, it's a good thing to know and is still applicable here.

You will need to be patient with yourself over the first 12 months, as you wait for your body to heal, recover and stabilise. However, there are things you can actively do, to assist this recovery process.

Taking care of your own health and fitness, will help you recover much faster – and get you back on your horse more easily!

So, there are a few parts to this. And you will need to heed any medical advice you receive. But here are some basic rules to follow – and I promise this chapter will be short and sweet – with no extreme dieting recommended(!).

Nutrition

Try and eat a healthy, sustaining, energy dense, and well-balanced diet. No matter how much you want to lose any baby weight, DO NOT starve yourself! You need plenty of quality protein, carbs, healthy fats and vitamins and minerals, in order to cope with the demands of a baby – particularly if you are breastfeeding.

If you need help – consult a nutritionist (often this can be free via public hospitals), or your Maternal and Childcare Nurse.

Alternatively, many women have great success going down the 'alternative' or 'natural' route when re-building their health and hormones post-birth. Naturopaths, Integrative GP's and the like are becoming more and more popular – and shouldn't be dismissed. I have personally discovered how beneficial this alternative approach can be – as often GP's and medical professionals will look strictly at diagnosable 'medical conditions' – rather than improving the quality of your health via the use of nutrition, herbs and supplements.

You can do a quick Google or Facebook search to find one in your local area – or simply visit your nearest health food store, as they will either have an in-store Naturopath or can recommend one.

One of the most powerful things that I have discovered (after my body completely crashed in my early 20's from high-stress corporate jobs!) – is how beneficial it can be to avoid or limit sugar!

Now stay with me here...

Sugar has been well documented to completely mess with your health. It can cause your blood sugar levels to go completely haywire and it can make you store and accumulate fat more easily. It can even make you really depressed and mess with your hormones.

Sugar can seriously do all sorts of undesirable things to your health – so do try to keep it to a minimum.

And I know, it is really hard, particularly when you are in the throes of baby sleep deprivation. And sugar is indeed addictive! Our bodies were originally designed to seek out sweet, sugary energy hits, to ensure our survival as a species (i.e. to be able to run from the hungry lion behind the bush over there!).

But whilst our lives have certainly adapted(!) – our bodies still have the addictive tendencies to get really hooked on sugar.

And yep, sugar can give you that quick energy pick-me-up that we often need when looking after kids! It certainly DOES make you feel good in the short term.

But what excessive sugar really does, is give you that short burst of energy for a brief time, and then sends your body crashing back down again. This becomes a cycle of sugar high, sugar crash, which trust me - leaves you feeling like crap and throws your entire body out of whack.

That said - the occasional sugar hit won't hurt too much – and should be enjoyed from time to time. Just make sure you don't become too reliant on it.

But be warned – if you do try to quit sugar, it can be really tricky because of its addictive nature. It is fairly similar to quitting nicotine or a drug, in that you will quite possibly experience withdrawal symptoms and feel like crap for a week or two. And often – the more you try your hardest to quit sugar – the more you tend to crave it. So it takes A LOT of willpower!

Caffeine can also be very tempting, and many mothers survive the first 12 months of a new baby with caffeine practically running through their veins! But be aware that it can cause issues for some sensitive babies if you are breastfeeding. And it also isn't healthy for your body long term. It quite often messes with your already messed up sleep patterns, which is something you really don't want. So coffee is always best in MODERATION!

Now I bet you are thinking – but it's the only way I can survive! I can't survive without sugar and coffee! And I hear you. And if you are desperate, some good quality, ultra-dark, lower sugar chocolate is great in small quantities. But trust me, you will cope better, with proper nutrition.

It will be a struggle at the start – but it gets easier – and you WILL feel better!

But don't freak out! You do not have to cut out carbs or fat or any other wacky recommendations from common diet fads that spread like wildfire across your Facebook feeds.

My best advice from my own experiences and research – is to simply JERF. Which means to 'Just. Eat. Real. Food.'

This simply means that you steer clear of too much packaged, processed foods.

Instead, you eat plenty of quality meat, fish, eggs, grains, veggies (lots of 'em) and fruit instead. Team your veggies up with a healthy fat, such as Olive Oil (as this is said to improve the nutrient uptake). And ensure you get quality carbs, in the form of pasta, rice, potatoes etc.

If you are vegetarian or vegan, ensure you get some protein from other sources – and I strongly recommend consulting a dietician in this case.

Basically – eat the way your grandparents most likely did! Traditional Sunday Roasts. Wholesome meals. Meat, veggies, eggs – REAL FOOD!

This approach to eating will also hopefully rub off on your children as they grow up – which makes you a brilliant mum! Score!

Next, if there is one thing I can absolutely recommend – it's asking your doctor to check your basic vitamin and mineral levels post-birth! Particularly both your Iron levels and Vitamin D.

Often after childbirth you can get really low in Iron (due to blood loss during the birth, and the fact that your baby will often drain your reserves during pregnancy etc). This can really affect your energy levels – and leave you feeling completely worn out. The times I've ended up low in Iron – it's been really amazing to feel the difference when you finally realise and start taking supplements. All of a sudden you can go from feeling like your operating through this exhausted haze – to actually becoming much more alert and energetic.

The other main one I recommend you get checked is your Vitamin D levels. This is very often overlooked but can make a huge difference to your mood. It's becoming increasingly common for many of us to be Vitamin D deficient, particularly during Winter, when you're not out in the sun much – and particularly if you spend a fair chunk of time inside without much sunlight.

Trust me – Vitamin D can be a real 'happy pill' because without it – your mood drops through the floor and life becomes a struggle. I'd even go so far as to say that there was a time in my early 20's after a long period of stress and a corporate lifestyle, that my low Vitamin D levels resulted in me being quite depressed (and this was later confirmed by a GP). So get it checked!

Finally – ensure you stay hydrated! As most health care professionals will tell you – this is crucial particularly if you are breastfeeding (and bubs is sucking you dry like there is no tomorrow!).

Dehydration makes you feel really crappy. So try and keep water bottles located around the house, so they are within easy reach. If your baby has a habit of falling asleep on top of you (like mine certainly were), make sure you have a drink bottle next to the couch.

It honestly is a simple recipe for success – but you will need to be determined to make this happen.

Stay strong there Mumma!

Fitness

For the first few weeks, walking between your bed, your babies cot, the couch, and the toilet is quite possibly all the activity you will require(!). But as time passes, it is a great idea to begin gentle exercise, even if it is simply putting baby in a stroller and walking to the letterbox and back (depending on how far away your letterbox really is!).

The key here is to build yourself up slowly – and always consult with trusted medical professionals for advice.

If you are lucky enough to have a mothers group, or friends you can team up with, it's always much nicer to go walking together.

Meet up somewhere, like the local park, let the kids socialise and play – whilst you get some fresh air and exercise.

Be patient, be gentle and be kind to YOURSELF!

Don't try to move mountains too soon that you end up jeopardising your recovery. Or making yourself feel worse.

And keep it relatively enjoyable! Don't traipse around in the freezing cold and mud because you simply feel you MUST exercise. Choose to walk happily (and warmly!) around the local shopping centre instead!

If dancing interests you – find a fitness dance class for adults, or Adult Ballet – or something along those lines.

If you enjoy swimming – try doing that!

If you want to combine your fitness and exercise with that of your horse – put your horse on a lead rope and take him/her for a walk/run WITH you!

Just do whatever works for YOU!

Weight loss

Many mums tend to put on a reasonable amount of weight during pregnancy – and then put themselves under immense pressure to lose the 'baby weight' immediately after birth.

This is not a good move!

If you put yourself under too much pressure you will most likely end up very miserable.

Baby weight takes a little time to shift and it's not as big a deal as most women are made to feel.

This is where you MUST turn a blind eye to the skinny Celebrity photos that fill the magazine stands and your Facebook feeds.

Skim right past those super-hero women who pop up on Facebook who may be positively glowing and fitting straight back in to their bikinis 2 weeks after popping out a child.

Congratulate the competitive, professional horse-riding women who DO indeed end up back on the horse competing a mere few weeks after childbirth – but know you do not have to do that (and in most cases I'd say it was darn right silly – as there would have been no way in hell I would have 'jiggled' my 'lady-bits' that soon after!).

DO NOT COMPARE YOURSELF TO ANYONE! YOU ARE YOU!

Your journey is unique – and you are not a 'lesser' person for being a different weight or size.

Whilst yes of course – you do need to do your best to be a **healthy weight** that is appropriate for your height and build – please take things slowly and heed medical advice that is specific to your situation.

If you do want to – or get advised that you NEED to lose some weight – get some expert advice and support. Please don't starve yourself – nor over-exert yourself.

Be ok with where you are – and just aim to look after your health as much as you can manage.

Strength

One of the other main frustrations for us 'Horsey Women' is the muscle tone and physical strength we tend to lose after having babies.

As we all know, our core-strength is vital for our riding positions and balance. And as us mums would also know – you pretty much lose this core strength COMPLETELY after kids.

For me, one of the weirdest feelings post-birth was that feeling of 'empty space' through your middle or tummy. Once baby has vacated the area and is busy making himself/herself known on the outside of your body(!) – you feel like you have nothing! No core, no tummy, just empty space within you.

Many of us may also be a tad flabby and floppy around the middle too!

This is normal though and something you CAN regain in time through the appropriate exercises.

It's best to consult an expert who can help you with the appropriate exercises that are RIGHT FOR YOU. Whilst I'd love to give you the instant, easy solution to recovering your core strength post-babies – there is no one size fits all answer!

A good place to start would be to see a good Physiotherapist. They can assess your body and make recommendations.

Otherwise Pilates has been well-proven to be hugely beneficial for riders – along with Yoga. You might like some kind of Gym program – whether it be weights or fitness/toning classes. Or there are some programs around who use Dance as a form of fitness and strength – if you want to do something a bit more light-hearted and fun.

'Barre' classes have been derived from Ballet – and are becoming increasingly popular – and are incredibly effective at toning and strengthening your body.

And if public displays of fitness just aren't your thing – luckily these days the internet provides private opportunities a plenty!

There are stacks of health and fitness programs online that you can join which offer you video-recorded exercises to follow – that you can do in the comfort of your own home. You should even be able to rustle up some specific post-baby exercise programs too.

Do some 'Googling' and see what you can find.

Sarah Walkerden

CHAPTER 6:
Returning to Riding

Go Slow!

At three months you may well feel up to riding again. If so – great! Just get your doctors approval first.

If you don't feel up to riding – don't despair. There are no rules here. You do not have to ride if your body is still recovering, you don't have the energy, it doesn't feel right, or you just can't be bothered.

Baby raising can be really hard, so don't beat yourself up or give yourself a hard time.

But when you do feel physically and mentally ready to get back on your horse – do so wisely. Keep in mind that your body has changed, your hormones have changed, and your mental and emotional capacity has potentially altered.

So the absolute Golden Rule here is – GO SLOW!

If you have a quieter horse, this is a good option. But try to have some support on the ground. If your husband is not into horses, try and enlist a trusted horsey friend or an instructor.

Start small and build back up slowly. Do not expect to pick up where you left off before pregnancy and the birth of your child. It won't necessarily feel or be the same.

You may find that simply getting on your horse and riding for a few minutes at a walk is all you can manage to begin with.

Rebuilding your riding muscles, fitness and the fitness of your horse will take time.

If you have a younger horse, or one that is slightly more challenging, particularly after limited work – it can be a really idea to send them off to a trusted trainer or friend, who can give them a little 'refresher course' to get the 'yippies' and 'yahoooos' out of the way – before you get on. Particularly if you aren't feeling confident!

And then there are the sheer logistics of juggling a baby and finding the time to ride. And once you have multiple kids - it gets even harder.

So here goes...

Finding the time – the hardest thing of all!

If your husband works full time, and you are on your own, for much of the time, it can be really tricky to find ways to ride.

In summer, with daylight savings, you might be able to squeeze a ride in after hubby comes home from work. But then of course, it's usually witching hour with your beautiful baby, so it may or may not work – as quite often during these times daddy just isn't enough(!).

In winter, it's pretty damn hard. And if you are a single mum – I am in complete awe of you!

Weekends tend to be somewhat easier, IF you have a husband who is at home on weekends.

(I did not – mine worked weird hours, and generally, MOST weekends - which really sucked!)

But if you do have hubby home at weekends, a great idea can be making a deal with said lovely husband, so that he can do what he needs to during part of the weekend (maybe that's a couple of hours to play golf or football), and he then freely (notice that word gentleman!) gives you time, WITHOUT guilt, to play ponies. Tis only fair right?

However, it can send you a little stir crazy, looking out the window at your horses (or dreaming about them if they aren't at home with you), holding a baby during the times your husband or any other available help, isn't around to assist.

So, I have put together a few ideas which may enable you to squeeze in some extra precious horsey time.

Some of these might work for you and your child – whilst some of them sure as hell won't. So be prepared for failure here – and a fair amount of trial and error. Try not to get discouraged on the first attempt either.

You may need to work out the optimum timing for your child/ren – in order to achieve the greatest results.

And as we all know with our little darlings, what works one day, may not work the next!

The Stroller/Porta Cot/Play Yard Method

In reasonable weather, you can look at setting up your child in either a stroller or pram (with child well strapped in!) – and park it next to the arena or area that you ride. Obviously this won't allow you to jet off on a trail ride, but it can at least get your bum in the saddle, for maybe five minutes.

If this simple solution works for your baby or toddler – wahoooo! But you may find their happiness, only lasts for that brief five minutes, before they start screeching for attention.

It really does depend on the nature and temperament of the child, as to whether this works for any great length of time. If you have a fairly easy-going child, then it just might work, at least whilst they are little. But if you have more demanding babies (or a toddler) like mine were, it might not be so great.

Both my kids would possibly sit there for maybe two whole minutes, before starting to grump, wriggle and then scream blue-murder until the entire district knew I was attempting a ride.

So if the stroller doesn't work, or stops working as your child gets older, the next thing to try is to set up either a porta cot, or play pen, next to the arena (or the area you ride in). This obviously provides them with a little more freedom to move, whilst still keeping them contained and safe.

Just make sure you provide shade, water and a snack, and check for ant nests nearby or underneath(!). A picnic rug or similar can be placed down on the grass, so they aren't on prickly grass. Then it's just a matter of providing plenty of interesting toys – throwing them in – running to grab your horse – crossing your fingers and toes – and hoping for the best!

On some occasions, this might buy you a magical 10 minutes of riding. If you are lucky it might be half an hour.

One thing's for sure when doing this - you tend to get VERY FAST at saddling up!

The Handy Neighbour Method

This one doesn't take too much explaining.

If you have a lovely neighbour (cue the lovely local older ladies), either right next door, or within the immediate vicinity, they might not mind coming around occasionally to play with baby for an hour, whilst you ride.

If your neighbour is baby obsessed, all the better!

You might like to see if you can do some kind of 'swap' system – so you might provide them with something in return for an hours babysitting.

Or if you're really lucky, you might have a capable teenager in the district who you can throw $20 at, to 'coo' over your baby for a bit.

The Child Swap

You might find you have a friend or acquaintance, with babies or kids at a similar age to you, who also wants to ride their horse, attend a yoga class, or just go shopping alone.

Sarah Walkerden

Why not ask if they might like to trade childcare? By this I mean, they look after your child whilst you ride, and then you repay the favour by looking after their child, whilst they enjoy some time off.

Mums MUST band together! If you can find some like-minded mums, and form an unofficial playgroup or similar, you might find this gives you with a tiny bit of freedom (not to mention you and your kids the valuable chance to socialise!).

Of course, you need to find other local mums who you trust and get along with, and all your kids need to get along fairly well too.

But it can be a really good system if you can find your 'tribe' and make it work.

The Magic Mum or Mother-In-Law Method

As the name suggests, most mums and sometimes mother-in-laws, are more than happy to spend as much time as possible with their grandkids.

I have always been really lucky here, as MY mum (although non-horsey) understands my need for horsey time. And as my husband and his sisters have always had horses, my mother-in-law has always been very supportive and encouraged me to ride, whenever they have been around.

So if they offer help – GO FOR A RIDE!

Just run – and don't look back!

The Child Care Method

Ok. So now you are desperate. You have no friends in the local vicinity, your mother-in-law lives three hours away, your husband has been working sun up to sun down for the past 3 weeks, and you NEED. TO. RIDE. NOW!

Consider childcare. I know it can be scary. I know it might seem like you are abandoning your child. But you aren't. Childcare, in my book, is wonderful. You pay people, who love babies and kids, to look after yours. Your child gets to socialise and to learn. They get a change in pace. And you get SPACE.

There are a few options with childcare.

The first, is Occasional Care. Often local councils, or family centres, offer occasional, casual childcare, for an hourly rate. You can book them in a day or two in advance, for as little as two hours, or for half or a whole day.

If it's your first time using childcare – this can be really handy as you can do a test run, to see how it works for both you and your child. Drop them off for two hours, go shopping and have a coffee, and come back. Consider it as 'dipping your toes in to the childcare waters'.

Obviously, there will be tears, from both child and YOU! Don't fight it, it's normal. But as with anything, practice makes perfect, and both of you CAN and WILL adjust.

And luckily for us exhausted mums – most childcare workers are simply amazing at helping to ease the drop-off process (and will cheerfully prise your child off you – as you dart out the door!).

(Of course if you have already returned to some form of employment – then childcare may not be as much of a mystery to you!)

If you find you need some more regular assistance, such as a whole day of freedom, each week, then a permanent booking at a childcare centre might work well. This is the most common form of childcare and offers regularity and routine for both you and your child.

If a large childcare centre doesn't sit well with you, you also might be able to track down Family Day Care. This is where your child is cared for by a childcare provider, in their own home. So basically, like a friend or grandmother, but a paid for service. Contact your local council to find a carer near you.

Personally, we started off with Family Day Care, and initially it was great for our first son, when he was little – particularly as our work schedule was unpredictable month to month and Family Day Care provided more flexibility. But as he grew, we found it wasn't such a great fit. Nothing wrong with the family day care provider – our son just wasn't clicking with her kids. So we found our local Day Care Centre, and never looked back.

And for those of you who feel guilty at even the thought of palming your child off to Childcare, please don't. There are many huge benefits for your child to attend a Childcare centre. Your kids will get the chance to find their own strength and independence away from you. They get the opportunity to learn to socialise with other people and other children. They get to play with new and exciting toys which they will love!

And Childcare Educators are brilliant – they teach your child cool stuff! For example, my two-year-old daughter, came home one evening last year, and suddenly she could count to five (and my husband and I nearly fell off our chairs when she started counting the bars on her cot!). Childcare also do all the 'messy' stuff that can be tricky or just plain annoying at home, such as finger painting and crafts.

On a developmental level, my first son was a pretty shy little kid. Over a little bit of time, childcare helped bring him out of his shell, and grew his confidence rapidly, with the support of the lovely ladies. He made lots of friends and even did their kinder program – which he loved (and so did we as it was so convenient with the availability of the longer hours!). He has since flourished at his first year of school this year – with an air of confidence that has quite surprised me!

For our daughter, she has always been incredibly energetic. More energetic than I could ever cope with. And when I say the word 'energetic' I mean it! She cannot sit still for longer than a minute or two. Yet she thrives at childcare! She is now three and goes four days a week. She loves going and is as bright as a button when she comes home. It gives her the activity and stimulation that she needs.

Sure - there are often tears to begin with. Once they (and you) adjust however, it can be the best thing ever!

And don't forget, there are Government subsidies for official childcare providers. Whilst it might seem expensive, the Childcare subsidies, can really help ease the financial pain.

These however are just a few ideas for getting in your precious riding time. There are possibly plenty of other ways too, so it's a matter of experimenting with your kids and horses and seeing what works for ALL of you the best.

Asking For Support

Now this can be the tricky bit. In order for you to continue on with your horses and get back in to riding after kids – you WILL need support around you.

First off – if you have a husband or partner who isn't horsey, it can be really tricky enlisting his support as he may not understand the emotional need you have within you – to have horses!

So my best advice, is to firstly – hand him this book! Encourage him, hell, BRIBE him to read it – as it just might help things.

Secondly, if he enjoys complaining about the expense, the effort, the endless trips with trailers for hay – you may need to just sit down with him and explain as best you can just how important horses are to your mental wellbeing.

Tell him you'll be absolutely batty and cranky without those cute furry ears, and tickly whiskers!

I do find that often us women do tend to just assume that our husbands understand our needs – without actually telling them. But in most cases – men just don't read our minds – and need to be told very precisely and concisely (no offence intended guys!).

If you have other family members who also have the tendency to question our need for horses – it might also be necessary to have a similar conversation with them.

Unfortunately you will always find people around you who may well remain unreasonable.

But I do know that if your family and friends support you and you KNOW you have that support – you are much more likely to be successful with your riding-after-kids endeavours!

CHAPTER 7:
Mummy Mindset Basics

Motivation & Energy

Ok, so now we are getting down to the nitty gritty issues that mothers often face mentally and emotionally when trying to get back in to horses.

And often the difference between a mum who succeeds in getting back in to horses – and a mum who doesn't – all comes down to learning about and implementing some mindset strategies.

So the first challenge is being able to fight through the 'mummy exhaustion' and find both the motivation AND the physical energy to get back on the horse.

Let's talk MOTIVATION.

Often when we are going through the early days with a new baby, or just through a difficult and more tiring phase of child-raising (such as teething, illnesses, nightmares, toddler tantrums etc!) – our motivation to do anything that requires physical effort can be really quite low.

And when you have a break from anything – including riding – we can quite often lose our 'mojo'. Meaning getting started on anything is tricky – as we have to force ourselves to do it.

Usually you find though, that the more you do of something – the more you want to do it. But getting started is always the hardest part.

And sometimes no matter how much you love a particular activity – such as riding(!) – it's so much easier to not do it, then to put the effort in to getting started.

Knowing this fact though can actually help you to push through this initial starting point pain, to allow you to regain your mental (and physical) momentum.

So do know that at times you are going to have to pull out some serious positive 'self-talk' to convince yourself to get out there and ride!

And then there is the ENERGY factor.

When you are so dog tired that even lifting your head off your pillow is a struggle – finding the energy to put one foot after another to exercise or ride is really tough going.

And that's ok! There will be times when you just don't have the energy to ride, and on really rough days it is much more sensible to simply take it easy, take all pressure off yourself, and just rest (as much as your child and your lifestyle will let you!).

Other days though, it is actually hugely beneficial to force yourself through the exhaustion and get outside and hang with your horse anyway. Even if you just go cuddle him in the paddock.

Because spending that time with your horse will always make you feel happier, lighter and more at peace with the world. And when your mood lifts – magically - so does your energy levels. Hurrah!

Know that spending time with your horse will equal more energy.

Even if it's just a tiny bit.

And that energy will then help you tackle the rest of your day with slightly more enthusiasm.

The Things Horses Teach Us

Here's something I've learnt in the last 18 months or so, in my own journey getting back in to horses with my brand new, young, Off-The-Track Thoroughbred, 'Trigger'.

Your horse WILL show up all your flaws.

Depressing huh?

But I can provide you with hope here.

In order to successfully work with and ride your horse/s you need a few things.

You need to BE IN THE MOMENT!

You need to be emotion neutral.

You need to leave your problems at the paddock gate – and separate your horse time from the stress within the rest of your life.

Your horse needs a firm, clear, consistent leader.

So you need to do things and ask things of him in the same way, each and every time.

You need to be firm and assertive – without getting angry, frustrated or MEAN!

Can you see how clearly a horse can demonstrate your potential flaws – and play on them?

As women – and stressed out mothers – we tend to get emotional, tired and just a little bit grumpy from time to time. Right?

If you keep those yucky feelings unchecked inside you when dealing with your horse – things so often go pear shaped.

You might have a tendency towards frustration and anger when your horse doesn't do what you have tried to ask of him.

Or you might get timid and scared (whether you realise it or not) when your horse does something silly.

Sarah Walkerden

There comes a time where your horse will teach you these valuable lessons.

He/she might appear too timid and might shy at every possible thing.

Or they might become aggressive. Or just plain 'shitty' or grumpy.

And in order to move forward with your horse in a positive manner – you WILL need to learn to control these emotional reactions within yourself – before you can help your horse.

Have I freaked you out yet?

Self-awareness can be really scary when you start to recognise what your horse is trying to teach you or expose in you.

For me – it was a deep-seated fear – and total self-doubt. My darling Trigger showed me just how much my fear was damaging our relationship and holding back our potential success.

At first when I really started to realise this I fell in a miserable heap. Understandable right? It's hard when you realise that the problems you are having with your horse is really a problem that's coming from within you – and your lack of something – whether it be a lack of riding skill, a lack of understanding horse behaviour, a lack of patience, or a lack of confidence.

But the cool thing is that when you do actually become aware of the things that are happening within yourself – you can find ways to fix them!

Hoorah!

There is very little in this world that can't be solved.

And I am now at a point where I firmly believe that horses and learning to work and ride them successfully – is as much of a personal development journey – than a mere 'riding' or 'horse ability' journey.

So whether you are struggling with anger, frustration, timidness, fear, lack of timing, lack of 'feel', or you're just unable to read your horses behaviour and demeanour effectively enough – it doesn't matter.

Because I also firmly believe that everything is fixable.

Solutions can be found.

So whilst yes, self-awareness can be slightly painful when you come to admit that you have some short-comings.

It means you CAN actually do something positive to improve the situation – and improve you!

Trigger has forced me to really STEP UP and get firmer and clearer with my requests. I'm learning to read him more closely and more quickly – and react faster and more appropriately – to get better results with him.

But I haven't done it alone.

I'm lucky enough to have a horsey husband who has the ability to help me teach Trigger cool stuff (Just not the passion to train horses for himself anymore).

But alas, he aint so great at teaching people (particularly me!) and being a confident male who has never really experienced any self-doubt when it comes to horses – he hasn't always understood my fear.

Which is where I then have forced myself out of my comfort zone and floated Trigger to several horsemanship clinics, to get hands on help from a professional trainer.

I've also joined a few online confidence programs to learn as many mindset strategies as I can to re-wire my thoughts and emotions.

(For anyone interested, please look up Jane Pike and her Confident Rider online courses. Jane's strategies are amazing and well worth the very small investment to join 'Joy Ride').

Sarah Walkerden

And all of this has caused my confidence to not only grow in relation to communicating more effectively with Trigger – but it also has had a flow on effect on the rest of my life.

I'm running our businesses more confidently – and embracing life with a new-found confidence that has been catapulting our success.

Interesting hey?

Our horses show up our flaws – and then help us to fix them. And finding and fixing these issues within ourselves – can seriously make us better people in every single aspect of our lives. Including making us better mums (or parents!).

Woweeee.

If that isn't a good reason to continue on with horses after having kids – I don't know what is!

And I really hope I haven't scared you or blown your mind too much.

But I think it's really important to try and recognise what our horses are trying to show us.

When you really deep dive in on your issues with your horses – and figure out what it is within yourself that you are struggling with – it gets super fascinating trying to figure it all out.

I find myself wanting to learn more and more and more!

And then seeing how learning all these mindset strategies actually has an impact on my horse and his behaviour.

Add to that the puzzle of learning how to effectively communicate with your horse – and improving your horsemanship and riding skills – and I don't know about you – but the whole challenge of conquering it all just has me hooked.

So there is something for you to think about.

Becoming self-aware is scary and often depressing. And it's ok to wallow a little.

But then you need to come out fighting – and figure out what, how and whom can help you to overcome these issues.

And that indeed is where the REAL fun begins...

The Power of Positive Thinking

It's super easy for us to get caught in a trap of negative thought patterns.

And this is also tied in to the above section about what horses can teach us.

When things go wrong it's easy to dwell on that feeling.

Yet generally there is a positive that you can gain from each negative situation you encounter.

And training yourself to find the 'gold nuggets amongst the horse poop' can be a really powerful thing.

Because when you start seeking out the positives – you start to seek out the solutions, and in that way you can continue to move forward.

If you dwell on the negatives, you're just not going to get very far. You'll stay stuck down a very dark rabbit hole.

So if there is one thing I can share with you - is to try to find the sunny side to things.

If you fall off your horse in to a puddle and get soaking wet – celebrate that you are still alive (hopefully with all bones still intact) to tell the tale (no matter how embarrassing it might seem!).

Sarah Walkerden

If after two months of perfect training and preparation – your horse prances his way sideways around the arena in your dressage test as 'high as a flippin' kite' – celebrate the learning opportunity he gave you.

Celebrate that you even got to the dressage arena!

Celebrate even the tiniest of little things that went right each day.

Your child learnt to count to five – wahoooo!

Your toddler stayed content in his stroller for a whole 10 minutes whilst you brushed your horse – hooray!

Find the gold – find the lessons – and seek to improve things in future.

Post-Natal Depression

The topic of Post-Natal Depression is one I take seriously – and even though this book has been intended to be light-hearted, this is a topic that I feel is important to zero in on.

Whilst I never got officially diagnosed with Post-Natal Depression when either of my kids were born – I honestly believe (and years later can now freely admit) that I was probably very borderline – particularly within those first 6 months.

I fought it off as best I could – partly because I was pretty darn determined to, due to having experienced depression within family members and friends.

But I also firmly believe that it was always my horses that saved me.

Having my horses force me to step outside in to the fresh air – and escape screaming babies and toddlers and a chaotic household – gave me time to breathe, release the stress and just chill the hell out.

My dreams of riding successfully, joining Adult Riding Club one day – and getting back to enjoying my horses again – kept me putting one foot after the other during the daily grind.

Having horses forced me to keep my body active. My brain to take a breather. And my mind to dream of future horsey plans.

Pretty powerful stuff this horse caper hey?

I honestly believe that horses give us 'horsey mums' a distinct advantage.

They provide that opportunity to escape – and allow us to feel human – and like we used to feel before kids.

They return us to who we really are – so we don't lose ourselves to the chaos of children.

And I don't pretend that having these extra 'beings' to look after doesn't cause some stress and difficulties.

Horses can make life more complicated – particularly when you're knee deep in newborn nappies.

But if you just hold on to your dreams throughout that early big dark hole – you'll come out the other side with at least some of your sanity still intact.

But as mentioned earlier, if you are ever struggling too much for too long, please do not hesitate in seeking help.

Get Social

Now, after that heavy bit, let's lighten the mood by letting you in on one of THE most powerful mindset, motivational and mood boosting activities out there. Getting social!

Getting out and about with good friends or close family does amazing things for your mindset.

Connecting with people who are either going through or have gone through the same challenges you have, or simply having someone to laugh with is highly under-rated and one of the simplest ways you can drag yourself out of a slump.

Sometimes hanging out with a baby, toddler or young kids day-in, day-out, can really drive you batty – and you absolutely do NEED to have some adult conversation from time to time.

If you can manage to drag yourself out of the house to a café, park, play centre or just someone else's home – this works even better!

The old saying – a problem shared is a problem halved – is totally accurate.

Share your challenges and feelings and you'll feel better. If you can find another mum or several with kids of similar ages, it can be super comforting to hear that they are going through exactly the same things.

And despite my recommendations earlier to avoid sugar and coffee like the plague – sometimes you can never quite under-estimate the power of the occasional cake, coffee and great company!

So any time you feel the need, make a phone call and get the hell out of the house to socialise.

Or if you really struggle to find anyone local who you can call upon – often many friends can be found online. Particularly if you need some other 'horsey mums' to chat to.

Which is why I have created the Horsey Mums Collective – but we'll talk more about that later.

CHAPTER 8:
Riding Confidence (or lack-there-of)!

It is not uncommon for mums to find that they lack a hell of a lot of confidence, post-babies, when it comes to their riding and horses. Children are a massive responsibility, and the thought of putting ourselves in danger, and leaving them without your care, is pretty darn petrifying.

If this happens to you, please don't stress out or worry too much about this. It's completely normal and happens to even the strongest riding women among us.

You can overcome this sudden fear or lack of confidence simply by taking baby steps towards your goals and by enlisting help where necessary.

For me, I was a bit of a nervous nelly before kids anyway. And I actually found that I was more confident AFTER kids. In my mind, after suffering through long and harrowing natural births, with practically zero drugs (stupid me!), I figured if I could do that – then riding was a piece of cake.

But despite the fact that thought was in my head logically, I have still struggled. Partly due to the internal thought processes and beliefs I've held about myself since I was a child.

But I have found a couple of things that can really help in this area.

Firstly, be patient and kind to yourself – and don't ever give up. A lack of confidence is completely normal. More people suffer from it, than you might realise. Even those of us who appear outwardly confident women, can tremble in our boots just thinking about getting on a horse. Even when you WANT to get on your horse. Even when you love it!

Recognise that it's an internal mental process, as well as physical, to get yourself back up and riding again.

Secondly, get help, guidance and support. If you have a riding instructor – perfect! If not, get one! If your horse isn't quiet enough, find a riding school or instructor who has a quiet schoolmaster.

I discovered the value in this just recently. I have been battling my confidence issues, with my young Thoroughbred. He is quiet, for a young horse, but still green, and therefore presents a challenge.

And I have been feeling a little rusty, unbalanced and uncoordinated, after not having ridden much for so long.

So I went for a riding lesson, on a quiet schoolmaster, on the lunge. And it was brilliant! It allows you to work on you, without having to worry too much about what the horse is doing.

Thirdly, go slow. Really slow! I mean slower than you ever thought you could go. What do I mean?

Well, it's all in the baby steps. And no, not your child's steps, YOURS!

If all you do, is put the saddle on, do some ground work, put your foot in the stirrup, take it out again, and then quit – then that is a massive step in the right direction.

Set Yourself A Plan

If the 'fear bug' hits you, my advice is to set yourself a bit of a plan, with some tiny goals, which will inch you towards getting back on and riding.

Don't feel like you just need to get the hell over it and jump straight on. You can totally break it down into much tinier tasks which inevitably makes things far less daunting.

For example:

Step 1: Basic Groundwork (Leading forward, stepping backwards, yielding hindquarters).

Step 2: Basic Lunging (Go, Stop, Trot, Stop, Change Direction, Stop – all with a nice attitude and calmness)

Step 3: Put Saddle On – Do Step 1 & 2 Again!

Step 4: Saddle Up, Do Groundwork, Get Horse To Stand Next To Mounting Block

Step 5: All of the above – plus put foot in stirrup.

Step 6: All of the above – plus sit on horse for 30 seconds.

Step 7: All of the above – plus sit on horse for 3 minutes.

Step 8: All of the above – plus ask for 3 steps of walk.

Step 9: All of the above – Walk horsey around for a full five minutes (Go, Stop, Go, Change Direction).

And so on....

If at any your horse is unsettled one day, or you just don't feel strong enough, go back a step or two. You don't have to get on. It DOES NOT MATTER!

The important thing is, that you give yourself time, and go easy on yourself.

It doesn't matter what anyone else is doing with their horses.

Just focus on you, your horse, and feeling good again.

It can be incredibly frustrating, and incredibly disappointing when things don't go according to plan, but you need to try and train your mind to focus on the positives. And recognise that not doing something, that doesn't feel right, is not a failure. And in many cases, tends to be quite smart!

You might also find, that even with the best intentions, and a solid plan or goal in place, you might get to the time where you can escape the kids, and ride, but you have no energy.

This is ok and completely normal. Sit in the paddock, hug your horse, or even go to bed and catch up on sleep.

Kids are exhausting! So don't feel guilty. Trust your gut and intuition and listen to your body.

You already are a 'super mummy' – without pushing yourself to the brink!

Give yourself and your horse something tangible to focus on!

One of the coolest strategies that I've learnt lately, is the real value on setting up very specific tasks for both you and your horse to focus on and complete – as a way of diffusing potentially anxious situations.

Particularly if you are an 'English' rider like me, we quite often fall into the trap of simply trying to ride our horse in 20 metre circles, or just around the permitter of a riding arena (or paddock).

Yet if you are somewhat anxious and your horse is somewhat anxious – this can actually be a recipe for disaster.

If however you were to set up a basic obstacle course, maybe with a few cavelletti/jump poles on the ground, some witches hats (traffic cones), barrels or tyres – and then invent some specific tasks or exercises that you and your horse are going to complete – this becomes a much more successful strategy of riding and working your horse.

Why? Well, it provides for more focus. If you have a certain task (no matter how basic it is) to complete you tend to be forced to provide more clear, concise direction to your horse. And therefore – you ride better!

When your horse has to also concentrate on tackling various objects and exercises – it gives HIM more to focus on too. It helps to switch their brains on so that they have to pay more attention to you and what you are asking.

It also helps with desensitising and getting your horse used to different objects as well.

In fact, an extension of this might even be to put some commonly used baby items in the middle of the arena and allow your horse to get used to them whilst you ride around them. Think strollers and prams, baby walkers, bikes, toys etc.

This will make horsey-mummy juggling that little bit easier if you can prepare your horse in a low-pressure situation – in advance of trying to take your horse on a trail ride with hubby beside you pushing the pram!

Either way though, set yourself up with an obstacle course and have a clear plan in your head as to what you want your horse to do – and then see if you can get it done.

It might be to get your horse to circle around one barrel and then the next, in a figure 8 shape. It might be for them to back up through some jump poles on the ground in an 'L' shape. You might like to have objects on top of barrels – that you need to pick up and move around the arena with your horse.

Trust me – taking this approach is a much better idea than just trying to ride perfect circles – when you're struggling with confidence.

It also has the lovely added bonus of preventing your horse from getting completely and utterly bored!

Ride A Quiet Horse

If tackling your own horse/s scares the living daylights out of you, the best thing you can do is to find either a quiet lesson horse or schoolmaster to get your riding mojo back – or go on a quiet trail ride on a quiet trail riding horse.

This way, you can purely focus on yourself and prove that you can indeed survive riding once again. Learn to trust your own abilities and balance once more – without having to worry about a slightly challenging or difficult horse who may require more confidence from you.

I honestly can't recommend this to you as a worthwhile strategy enough (which is why it's been mentioned twice!).

The Mechanics Of Fear

Here is what I've learnt lately about fear. I'm hoping these basics will at least give you a starting point to help you overcome any fear you may have about horses AND anything else in your life as well.

'Fear' is ingrained in us as a warning sign to potential danger. It is useful from time-to-time and you should listen to this feeling when it occurs. If your horse feels like he wants to bolt or attempts to rear – and everything in your gut and body tells you that you SHOULD be scared – then you may actually want to listen to that(!). Do whatever it takes to defuse the situation with your horse, get off, put your horse away and seek some extra assistance. If you feel you do not have the ability or knowledge to overcome a dangerous behaviour in your horse – listen to that fear. It could well save your life!

However! Often our fear instincts kick in when our lives aren't actually in any danger. This is where you need to make a judgement call, become aware of that fear response within your body and go – 'thanks for that – but I don't need you right now'. Recognise it for what it is, push it to one side, let it go and continue on. Because the more aware of it you are – the more you realise you can control it.

Another cool thing to note, is that FEAR has the same (or fairly similar) physiological reaction within your body as EXCITEMENT. So whether you get butterflies in your tummy because you are excited about an event, you will feel pretty much exactly the same as when you feel scared about an event. Knowing this is pretty cool. Because when you become aware of those 'fear' thoughts entering your head, you can then choose to switch it around and tell yourself that it's excitement instead.

Which leads to this. Often we think of fear as being a negative thing. That we must be hopeless if we are scared of something when other people are not. That we should work towards eliminating fear in all aspects of our lives. Not true at all!

Firstly, fear or nervous tension before an event means that you CARE about the outcome. That's a good thing – as it helps us to perform better. Secondly, the fear response in our bodies creates a surge of adrenaline. If you get really good at becoming aware of the fear that rises within you before going out to ride your horse etc – you can then actually redirect this extra energy within your body, towards the task you wish to perform or achieve. Cool right?

You can essentially use your fear to fuel your fire! You can learn to manage it so that it assists you in going further – rather than stopping you. Hooray!

Learn Everything You Can About Mindset & Mental Strategies

One of the most powerful things I have done to improve my confidence is by learning as much about mindset as I possibly can – in an effort to become more in control of my own thoughts, emotions and feelings.

There are soooooooooo many strategies you can learn and employ to help you overcome any type or level of fear imaginable.

And generally even just understanding where your negative thought patterns are stemming from and that you do actually have the power to turn it around and control how you think – can make the world of difference.

Now I am not about to tell you that I am expert here. I can only go on what I've learnt and experienced.

So if you really feel you need some expert help to overcome your confidence issues and fear, here are a few experts who may be able to help – as they specialise in helping horse riders to both overcome fear in general – and achieve their riding and competitive goals.

All three of these ladies are absolutely brilliant!

Jane Pike
Confident Rider

Natasha Altoff-Kelly
The Riding Success Institute

Tanja Mitton
Equestrian Success & Mindset

CHAPTER 9:
Clutter Clearing Your Way Towards Success

Now this particular chapter might make you wonder about my personal sanity.

But I can assure you that us mums can make powerful changes to both our emotional and mental state – and therefore the rest of our lives – simply by sorting out our physical 'crap'.

And yep we all hate housework. We hate cleaning. It's completely boring sorting through endless piles of kids clothes and toys.

Yet once it's done we really do feel awesome.

I know it – and YOU know it – that having a whole stack of junk and mess and chaos around us – really drags our energy down and makes us feel completely overwhelmed.

So if you are struggling to find the motivation and energy to get back in to horses (or struggling with life in general!) – this can be a very powerful place to start.

And I really felt this topic seriously deserved an entire chapter to itself.

Because instead of trying to tackle your mental or emotional issues head on – you'll quite often find that when you are feeling low – your physical environment in which you live will be reflectively chaotic as well.

So why not tackle the mess – in an effort to help lift your mood?

It's seriously so much easier to tackle little bits of the mess around you – than beating yourself up over your mental 'stuckness' or 'low mood'.

The question often is however – where on earth do you start? How on earth do you approach sorting out a humungous mess when it all just seems to hard and completely overwhelming!

The answer is to have a very simple plan of attack, tackle small sections or 'spots' at a time, break it in to smaller tasks – and put one foot in front of the other.

Which is what we will tackle in this very next section...

Tackling Tiny Areas At A Time!

Yep – the best way to start clutter clearing is by picking one tiny little spot within your house – that truly annoys the heck out of you – and fix it!

As with anything, breaking a massive task, down in to more manageable bite-sized chunks, will make the clutter clearing task much less daunting or overwhelming.

If your entire house has become completely out of control – you may even like to write down a list of rooms – and then areas within each room – that you need to tackle, so that you can start ticking them off one-by-one.

For example! You may wish to start with your dining room table. Often dining room tables become a dumping ground for physical mail and paperwork.

Or at least this is true for us, as we have quite a tiny two-bedroom house with very limited storage space.

You come home at the end of the day, and swing by your letterbox. You're tired, you're desperate for a cup of tea and some down time.

So you fling the mail you just collected on to that poor dining table, with the internal promise, that you'll deal with it later.

Or you might open it there and then to see what it is – discover it's a bill or a bank statement – which is totally boring or just beyond your current head space in that moment, so you fling it on to the dining table – again to deal with it later.

A week, two weeks, maybe even a month or two goes by, and the pile of paperwork on your dining table grows as you dump more mail on to it each evening.

If you like to sit down at your dining table each evening, you may even push the piles of paper to one end and eat at the other(!).

And suddenly you discover that your dining table is simply a mass of messy bits of paper and you have no idea what to do about any of it.

Sound familiar?

Or maybe you might be more organised than me AND my husband! If so – I take my hat off to you my friend!

But maybe it's the kids rooms, or the toys all through the living room – or that pile of clean washing that's built up on the couch, because you just haven't had time to put it away.

Whatever it happens to be for you – no matter how much you try to ignore it – this 'pile of crap' bugs you. Whether you are directly aware of it or not – mess and disorganisation weighs you down.

Physical clutter creates mental clutter.

So pick whatever that little spot is in your house that's been driving you nuts – and sort it, clean it, tidy it and deal with it.

Because once you deal with one tiny spot – I can just about guarantee that you'll feel better – and more inspired to tackle the next spot.

Before you know it - you'll feel happier, free, and more energised – and the horses won't know what's hit them.

Sound far fetched? Try it and see...

Tackle Your Horse Stuff

This might seem obvious but utilising this clutter clearing technique for motivating you towards riding – is really powerful.

Because no matter how exhausted, wrung out or just completely over life you are – when you sort out your tack room and horse gear – you'll truly feel more enthused about using it.

So if you discover that clearing out small sections of your house – and having it all neatly organised – has indeed made you feel better about life in general – it's then time to start sorting out your tack room, feed shed or wherever you use to keep your horse gear.

You can even take it one step further – and actually CLEAN your horse gear whilst you are at it.

Oil your saddle and bridle, and other gear such as breastplates. Buy and install some new hooks if needs be. Sort out all your brushes – and get rid of those miscellaneous and slightly weird leather straps that have been hanging around unused for like forever!

Put all your much-loved sparkly clean gear in their newly organised spots – and I guarantee it will make you feel so much better.

You'll be positively busting to pull your horse out of the paddock and get back in to the saddle – when your gear is so spiffy!

This also does give you the opportunity to suss out all of your horse gear. If you haven't used it in a little while after babies, you may find that you have broken or worn out gear hanging around. Going through what you do have allows you to assess the condition of each item and ensure you have a complete set of tack for each horse you need to ride.

If you need to replace anything – you can chuck it on your shopping list – and grab something new (or second hand) when you can, to ensure you have everything ready when you do want to ride again.

Or you might be able to arrange for some gear to be repaired.

You might however also find that using a little bit of shopping therapy can be well worth the effort (and slight expense!) in getting yourself motivated to ride.

A brand new blingy bridle or sparkly saddle pad might just be the ticket that motivates you towards summoning up your energy to get back on the horse.

Never underestimate the power of new gear and BLING!

Tackle Your Horse Clothing

Depending on whether you are an English rider, or Western, will determine what you feel the need to wear when riding.

For me – I've always ridden English, so breeches are a 'must-have'. But it could be your Wrangler jeans or just a certain pair of tights you feel comfortable in.

Whatever you used to ride in before children – will need to be reassessed. As unfortunately, no matter how well you survive pregnancy and childbirth, your body shape can change a little bit.

So you may need to check whether your riding clothes still fit or suit you.

I'm a size 8 (don't hate me – I've been blessed with super genetics!) – but even so a lot of my old joddies and breeches did not fit me quite as well after kids. Whilst extra weight wasn't much of a factor for me, there was still an extra bit of belly – and a slight widening of the hips(!).

And having the right riding gear that you are both comfortable and feel good about yourself in – can be really important in encouraging you back in to the saddle.

And I seriously get how tricky it can be to find the right riding gear that you feel good in. But this is where you really do need to force yourself to be super kind to yourself!

Sarah Walkerden

Plus there is so much range out there with riding breeches and clothing – that you should be able to find something that will do the job.

There are even some super-duper denim breeches these days that look just like skinny jeans – and these can be much more flattering for your post-baby figure if traditional breeches are just too daunting.

CHAPTER 10:
Goal Setting

So now we come to the magical topic of goal setting. It's a good one too, because without a goal, you really don't have a clue as to where you are going.

And learning how to set goals is useful for all aspects of your life as well as your riding. Having a goal, and a plan to get there will get you much further in life – than simply drifting along without purpose.

So I personally believe there are two main ways in which you can set goals.

The first way is where you dream big and set your ultimate, big, hairy, ambitious goal – and then break that goal in to smaller, more achievable steps.

The second way, which you may find easier to begin with, is where you take a smaller, more immediate and more easily achieved goal, and then tick that goal off – and then utilise the confidence you gain from that smaller achievement in order to inch yourself towards a bigger goal.

Now I've outlined both methods below, along with some other handy hints. However one of the most powerful aspects of goal setting – is actually writing it all down. It seems such a simple thing, but really can make a powerful difference.

Writing our goals and dreams down on actual paper (whether it's digital or physical) actually helps bring these things to life as they then exist in a physical form. It makes you much more likely to follow through and take action if you can regularly see, read or touch them – and writing your goals means you are making a commitment to yourself and to the universe(!).

Sarah Walkerden

The 'Big Dream' Method

This is where you may have already, or be able to come up with, an ultimate end goal that you would like to achieve. This might be reaching a certain level in Dressage or Eventing. Or it might be getting to the Olympics if you're really ambitious. Or it might be completing an 80km Endurance ride. Or a 'big dream' for you might be slightly more humble, such as getting to your first Grade 5 competition at Adult Riding Club.

The trick here is to pick something relatively huge - whether you believe it to be possible for you right now or not, and no matter how far away it might seem.

In fact I give you full license to give this a shot and really let yourself dream without limits.

It's amazing what you might come up with when you truly allow yourself to ponder the possibilities without worrying about the 'how' or the 'what-ifs'.

When you start to discover what it really is that you want – you can then progress on to visualising it actually happening in your mind. Do your best to picture yourself achieving whatever that crazy dream of yours is – and really see, feel, hear what it's going to be like once you are there. Immerse yourself in this imaginary experience.

Visualising in this way can be really powerful as it brings your dreams or goals to life – at which point you can begin writing it all down (or creating vision boards and the like), in order to make a firm commitment to it.

Once that's done – it's time to break it down in to more manageable steps and create the 'how'.

Break It Down

Once you have either one, or possibly several seemingly far-off dreams, it's time to break this bigger achievement down in to slightly smaller stepping stones.

To do this, simply brain dump every possible step, or thing you may need to do, in order to achieve your ultimate goal/s.

Consider the horse you may need to buy in future (or possibly the one you have is enough!), the gear and equipment you might need, the coaches you might need to invest in, and any other support you may need. And the things you need to be able to DO (such as flying changes, cantering a 20 metre circle, etc).

Once you have your initial list, you may find you can break each action step down even further, in to the tiniest of minute detail.

Develop a Timeline

Once you think you have written down everything you might need to do in order to achieve your goals, it's time to try and put these in some form of logical sequence (1, 2, 3 etc) and then plot it against a rough timeline.

Now you do need to look at this somewhat realistically. You possibly won't get to the Olympics in 6 months! But you also need to make sure you push yourself that little tiny bit, so that there is some element of pressure – and therefore more motivation.

It's a balancing act – and some of it will be guesswork – as you never quite know what life is going to throw at you.

Just do the best you can!

You might firstly break things down in to items to achieve over one whole year, and then each month, each week and finally each day.

The Start Small Method

If dreaming big just isn't something you are currently capable of right now in your current head space – that's ok! If you are in the midst of newborn hell or endless toddler tantrums – it can be really tricky to see what your future might look like in 6 weeks, let alone 6 months or 6 years.

And particularly if your confidence is fairly low, you simply need a basic starting point that doesn't feel too overwhelming.

So, the trick here is to pick a very small, relatively easy goal that you can achieve in the next week or month (depending on what you feel is best for you). It might simply to get on your horse and sit in the saddle for a minute or two. It might simply be to pull your horse out of the paddock and give him a jolly good grooming.

Think something really small, that would make you feel that little bit happier, and put a plan in place to get it done.

In order to get it done, you may need to organise some childcare or outside help. Or you may need to buy some new brushes for your horse – or get your saddle fit checked. List out the basic steps you need, write it down and start taking some small, daily action towards ticking those little things off your list.

Once you've got all your ducks in a row, you simply need to DO IT!

And then its celebration time! Pat yourself on the back whole-heartedly that you managed to achieve this goal.

You will hopefully find that this small start, encourages you to think slightly bigger. If you have now managed to groom your horse – maybe its time to start lunging or ground work. Tick that next bit off your list. If you managed to sit on your horse – maybe it's time to think about walking the entire perimeter of the arena.

Keep moving your 'goal posts' out slightly further each time and challenge yourself in little increments until you start to see some real progress.

Eventually once you gain some momentum with this, you will find that you start to dream bigger and bigger each time – until suddenly you feel like you can do and achieve anything you set your mind to.

Try it and see!

Daily & Weekly Routines

Regardless as to how you end up setting and achieving your goals with your horses and riding - once you know roughly where you are headed and in what timeframes, it's time to try and set yourself up with some daily and weekly routines and plans, in order to keep yourself moving forwards and set yourself up for success.

This will have to obviously fit in with your children's schedule, your work and any other lifestyle demands.

And you do need to allow yourself to be slightly flexible with it, as we all know that life and kids are rather unpredictable – and can throw us huge curveballs at any moment.

But if you can manage to set regular days and times when you can work or ride your horse throughout the week, it will help get you in to a rhythm.

You might also like to schedule in a little bit of daily exercise and some healthy socialisation. You may like to dedicate certain times of the day and week where you get your household chores done and time to spend with your kids.

Most importantly too – make sure you schedule in some down time or time to rest and chill out!

Getting a little more structure and routine happening within your day will not only help you and your kids to know what to expect and when – it prevents you from drifting through life and gives you more daily purpose and motivation.

It also takes a lot of the decision-making turmoil out of your lives which ends up saving you both time and mental energy!

If you'd like a sample daily/weekly routine schedule to print and fill out, you can find one here:
https://horseymumscollective.com/project/freebies/

Celebrate!

The most important and final step to goal setting and achieving – is to celebrate every tiny step forward that you manage to accomplish. As mums we tend to be very harsh on ourselves and we often forget to celebrate the tiny stuff. Yet as with the Clutter Clearing chapter, celebrating your wins and achievements really does help you to gain momentum and be inspired to keep moving forwards.

So if you manage to achieve something – tick it off your list – and celebrate!

You'll be positively smashing through those goals in no time!

CHAPTER 11:
Horsemanship & Training Battles

This book simply wouldn't be complete without a chapter on the topic of horse training itself. Because obviously regardless of what you do with your horses – and no matter what mindset techniques you employ – or how much you WANT to ride as a mum – often our horses have completely different ideas to us.

When we might envisage a nice quiet trail ride around the block, or a straight forward dressage lesson in the arena, or a nice day out at Adult Riding Club meeting new horsey friends – our horses' mindset, level of education AND willingness can make these 'simple dreams' of ours quite impossible.

Now earlier on, we mentioned a little bit about what horses can teach us. We touched a little bit on the journey you can go through and all the stuff you may need to face within yourself and LEARN in order to have success when working with a horse.

In this chapter I really want to highlight a few important things when attempting to 'train' and 'teach' your horse what you want from them – and how to step up to the plate to be the handler and rider that you need to be.

Now this is broken in to a few different parts – Psychology, Groundwork and Riding. I've done this to try and really highlight that the 'Riding' bit is just one component – as many of us 'English' riders who may have been bought up through the pony club or riding school ranks, don't always realise that many issues that we have in the saddle with our horses, can actually be solved through changing both our mindset and that of our horses, and through ground work.

Horsemanship itself is often a mis-understood term. Some of you may think it involves the kookier 'natural horsemanship' methods that have gained cult-like status over the past 10 years or so and instantly switch off to the idea as being somewhat 'fanatical' and 'far-fetched'. Some of you may simply believe that 'Horsemanship' refers to simply looking after your horse and knowing how to brush it and saddle it up (and without dismissing or appearing condescending of riding schools – this is where that concept generally comes from). Some of you might know exactly what I mean when I say the word 'Horsemanship' and some of you might already know and do this stuff without even realising it (if you're one of those lucky souls who find that intuitive horse training comes naturally to you!).

So, when I refer to 'Horsemanship' it means working with a horse in a way that makes sense to them. It means getting the basics established on the ground first – and it's simply a way of approaching how you teach a horse something (or anything!) that you wish them to do.

Now I will put in a caveat that I am in no way an expert on horse training nor a 'trainer', 'coach' nor qualified 'instructor'. But these are some of the basics that I've learnt along the way, to give you some insight on how to approach things and then where to get help if needed.

Psychology & How a Horsey Brain Works

Horses are herd animals, with a huge survival instinct as they are PREY. Out in the wild, they would be ever alert to potential danger such as mountain lions which may try to creep up and eat them(!). They are motivated by safety, comfort, food and company. And they are hard-wired to have a strong pecking-order.

The role of a dominant mare in the paddock, is to keep everyone else in the herd safe. The rest of the herd rely on this firm leadership and know to take their cues from her. So if the lead mare is relaxed – the whole herd is relaxed. If she takes fright and runs – the rest of the herd do everything in their power to follow her to safety.

Now much of this won't be too new to you. But it's important to understand these things so that we can establish ourselves in THEIR EYES that we are worthy leaders and worthy of their time and energy. We must be the ALPHA MARE!

It's important to be ASSERTIVE but not AGGRESSIVE in your approach however!

One of the most important things to realise is that horses are never 'out to get us', or to 'make us look silly' or any of those other human thought patterns that we sometimes believe our horses to think. Horses just don't think in that way. And its super important not to put our human emotions and thought patterns on to them.

Horses tend to live in the moment. They don't stand in their paddocks plotting elaborate schemes of how they are going to make our lives miserable. They stand in their paddocks eating grass. Full stop!

How you interact with them each and every time however, will determine what your horse thinks and feels about you. And horses do have good memories and will associate certain things or people with certain outcomes – such as a particular person who has treated them in a certain way.

Take the horse that may be difficult to catch as an example. If you are aggressive in any shape or form, either when you approach or when you handle and ride him – he may be fairly scared of you and run off. If you are timid, he might barge right in to your space and stand on your toes – or worse try to kick you. If you only ever go to catch your horse when you want something from him – such as work or riding – he may not be overly keen to see you either.

He's not just 'difficult to catch' or 'a bugger of a horse' for not wanting to be caught in these situations. There is generally a reason why he may be reluctant.

Sometimes yes – a horse just feels a bit frisky and cheeky and will try to 'have you on' in that moment. Or they simply may not feel like interacting with you at that particular moment. But this is where you must prove yourself as worthy in his eyes – and put the relationship between the two of you ahead of any of your desires.

The catching issue is just one example of an issue you may encounter. Some horses however may be a bit more subtle. Catching may not be an issue because they have learnt that they have no choice but to be caught. But their issues may be more obvious when being handled or under saddle, such as head tossing, pulling back when tied, the inability to stand still, shying, spooking, bucking etc.

The trick to working with a horse successfully is to be able to read what their behaviour is telling you, and assist the horse in feeling better about whatever situation you put him in. And then being able to teach him the right behaviours, with empathy, consistency and clarity.

You may have heard that you teach horses through pressure and release. You apply pressure to motivate the horse to do something – and then when they find the right answer (or do the desired thing) - you release that pressure, which lets the horse know he has done the right thing.

You then repeat the above to re-enforce the lesson, get it more solid, and fine-tune it (i.e. ask softer for more response from the horse).

One of the most important things however when teaching a horse anything is to look for calmness. There is no point forcing a horse to do something – or applying so much pressure to him that he spends all of his time reactive, petrified, explosive or just plain worried. A horse will not learn effectively if he is worried about his own survival.

It's also good to be aware that some horses are very stoic. Whilst many will wear their hearts on their sleeves and show you exactly how they feel (through bucking, rearing, stomping, tail swishing, shying and general histrionics!) – there are many horses who internalise all their stress, who may shut down and become robotic. These horses can appear quiet and safe on the surface, but in fact they can tend to be more dangerous as occasionally they can explode, seemingly out of nowhere. Or you may simply end up with a very dull and frustrating horse who never offers you any effort or enthusiasm.

So this is where experience and being able to read your horse is really important.

For the explosive, temperamental horse it's often easier to simply direct their focus and their feet into doing something constructive – which in turn will help settle them down. However you do need the confidence and ability to know how to do this! But reaching the shut-down horse can often be much trickier.

Many mis-communications can also occur between horse and rider/handler due to our own inability to offer clarity and consistency. You must be able to ask a horse to do something very clearly in a way that's easy for them to understand – and to do it the same way each and every time. Otherwise confusion will become a problem – and your horse will not become the willing partner you desire.

Finally, you must present each lesson to the horse in a way that allows him the ability to search for the right answer. And so that he knows there is, and he can find, an answer to anything that you ask.
Many horsemanship trainers call this developing the 'try' in your horse.

But again, if this mentality is new to you and you are struggling, please get expert help.

Groundwork

So now it's time to talk a little about ground work and ground manners. Because this was something I was never taught as a child, until I encountered some major issues with one of my horses and was rescued by a new found friend, who taught me the basics in my late teens/early 20's.

Often all we wish to do is ride – and we think that's all there is to horses. You just look after them – and then ride when you want to, right? Actually that's not quite the case. Making sure you can handle and communicate with your horse effectively and safely on the ground can make all the difference to how your horse feels and therefore behaves.

Firstly, having a horse who is easy to handle on the ground makes life for us much more pleasant. If you can catch, lead, tie up and saddle up without any dramas – life is much more simple.

And all of the behaviour your horse may display on the ground – certainly does transfer to how they behave under saddle. If you have a scared horse who is constantly uptight, pawing when tied and generally anxious – chances are you are going to get spooking and resistance under saddle.

And often it is so much easier to teach a horse certain movements and tricks from the ground, so that when you attempt these things under saddle the horse already knows the right answers – and then it simply becomes a matter of teaching them the corresponding correct aids from the saddle, rather than the ground.

Whenever you want to do anything with your horse you are looking for calmness, willingness and respect for your personal space.

Safety is everything here! No one enjoys handling a horse who drags along at the end of the lead rope in a world of his own – and no one enjoys handling a horse who barges right through you, who might kick, 'jig-jog' and pull you across the paddock etc.

And please be aware that each and every time you interact or handle your horse – you ARE teaching him SOMETHING! Whether you are aware of it or not.

Which leads us to one of the most important skills you can develop when handling your horse – LEADING!

Leading Your Horse

The importance of how well your horse leads should never be under-estimated. Different people and trainers do have different styles and ideas as to exactly where your horse should be in relation to yourself when leading. Some believe they should be right up next to you so that they are 'with you' and easier to control. Others believe it best to keep a horse slightly behind you, to ensure they have room to move in case of a fright, so you can react before they end up jumping on top of you.

I think in many cases it really depends on the type of horse you have and where that horse is at with his/her education. If you have a horse with the tendency to want to jump on top of you, barge in to your space etc –

then perhaps you may need to insist he stays a distance behind you, at least initially.

One important thing to note here too is that you don't need to hold the lead rope right under a horses chin – with a death grip! Often this is taught, or sometimes it's a natural instinct within us to try and control a horse by grabbing them firmly and insisting on this tight leading style.

However in a lot of cases this can lead to a horse becoming quite anxious – or possibly quite grumpy with you.

Instead, it's best to hold the lead rope more loosely, and possibly around half a metre down the rope. You want some contact with him, but your aim is to get him to relax on the end of the lead and stay with you – without you needing to use too much pressure.

If you want your horse to relax on the end of the lead rope – you need to relax! This 'death grip' style also tends to come from the desire to control your horses every move and prevent him from acting up. However unfortunately, even though it might seem instinctive for us, you do need to allow your horse that little bit of freedom and allow them to make mistakes, rather than prevent them. The ultimate aim with leading is to have a horse who is completely in-tune with you and what you're doing WITH ZERO PRESSURE on the lead. So essentially, they start to read you and your body language, rather than you having to even touch the rope.

It's also worth mentioning the value of using rope halters and longer, horsemanship or training style lead ropes. Whilst it might seem easier to use your stock standard wide, flat nylon webbing style halter that tend to be most common – these are not your best friend if you want to encourage communication and 'finesse' with your horse.

Horses can and will lean against the more comfortable pressure of flat, wide strapping. A rope halter is thinner and has more impact when you need more control – or simply offers more 'feel' and a more subtle, clearer communication to the horse. Just make sure you learn to use it fairly – and not as a torture tool.

Sarah Walkerden

A longer 12 foot lead also helps enhance the communication between your hands and your horses head – and gives you the ability to get your horse further away from you when needed, without letting go completely.

But regardless of what gear you choose to use (as it is personal choice!) – you do need to ensure you can get your horse to lead forward and backward with next to ZERO resistance.

Because when your horse is light on the lead rope, he tends to be calmer and more in-tune with you and your requests. He becomes more pleasant to handle. And issues such as float loading become almost non-existent, when your horse understands to come off the pressure on the lead.

This however is not a 'how-to' manual. To learn to lead a horse and teach your horse to lead – you will most likely require some professional help if it's something you're not familiar with.

There are some useful resources at the end of this book with suggestions on where to learn this.

Yielding

Besides being able to lead your horse forward softly and calmly – and being able to ask him to step backwards – being able to yield your horses body away from you (or toward you in some cases) is a very useful thing to be able to do.

It also helps ensure your safety – and that of your kids (if you ever have them around your horse).

Ultimately – you want your horse to yield to whatever you suggest to them THE INSTANT YOU ASK!

Because if you know you have control and influence over every single part of your horse in any circumstance, it will allow you, the horse and those around you to STAY SAFE.

So, you need to be able to yield your horses front-end, shoulders or forequarters away from you. And you need to be able to get him to yield his hindquarters away from you.

At first, you may teach this with some form of contact with the horse or a larger, visible aid or pressure, such as a swinging rope or pressure from your finger-tips. But the eventual aim is that one he yields from your slightest touch – and two that he can yield from your 'thought' or implied pressure.

You want this to where you can literally think 'move' and focus your attention on the part of your horse you wish to move – and he can almost read your mind and does just that.

Lunging

There are many different styles of 'lunging'. And unfortunately many of us get taught the wrong strategies and styles – or resort to thinking that lunging is only useful for exercise and wearing a horse out.

In horsemanship circles however, the art of 'lunging' is more about working a horses brain – than it's body. Yep for sure it does help exercise a horse, and in the end helps teach the horse to balance and use his/her body appropriately without a rider on top.

But the primary aim is to teach the horse various skills, such as smooth transitions and balance WHILST remaining CALM and RESPONSIVE to requests from the handler.

It also teaches a horse to move out and around you, and remain in-tune with you, whilst further away. Just remember that it's your horse that should be moving out and around you – not you moving around the horse! Quite often we fall in to the trap of allowing our horses to lunge us, without us realising it.

But I highly recommend watching Warwick Schiller to learn how to do this properly if that's of interest to you.

Sarah Walkerden

Riding

Ok, so now we are getting in to the fun part. And its important to know that all the work you do on the ground now needs to transfer to the saddle.

Ultimately – you want a relaxed but attentive horse who is willing to do as you ask and willing to learn.

But whilst on one hand you have the psychology and know-how to teach your horse to do the things that you want him to do – you also have the added complication of getting your own body to do what you need it to do as well.

In earlier chapters we've covered a little bit on fitness post-baby, muscle tone and strength (particularly your core), and riding confidence.

But this is the final piece of the puzzle – and that's actually being able to sit and ride your horse in an empathetic, well-balanced manner, with an independent seat and soft hands.

If you have a young or difficult horse, and your balance and riding ability just isn't what it used to be, please do get some riding lessons. You may be able to regain this strength and ability on your own horse – or you might need to make use of a quieter, well-educated school horse so that you can fully focus on your own riding skills.

And whilst many horses are relatively forgiving of our riding issues, many also are really not. So do be careful and honest about your own abilities and riding strength.

But the main things you should be able to do under saddle, is walk forward, stop, turn, yield his hindquarters, step his shoulders across, step back – and then do much of the same in/from trot and canter.

This can and does take a bit of time to master though.

It's also great to be able to navigate basic obstacle courses, and open and close gates from on top of your horse – and other such handy things.

Spending time ensuring you have the basics established with your horse will make life a whole lot easier as you attempt to advance your riding.

Establish The Basics Before Specialising

You may now be wondering, 'well all this horsemanship stuff sounds great, but what about my Dressage/Jumping/Camp Drafting/Endurance etc'. How do I do what I love using these principals?

The thing to know is that regardless of the discipline, the basics of riding are pretty much the same.

Once you have the basics established, you can then continue on to training for whatever specific discipline you desire – providing you train in a way that's empathetic to a horses needs at each stage.

Never let your competitive desires overtake your love and empathy for a how your horse feels. Don't attempt to shut down bad behaviour through force – simply find ways to work with your horse to make him feel better about what you're asking of him.

Not only will these suggestions help to keep you SAFE by producing a horse who can control his own emotions and look to you for guidance and support, but you might even get further than you ever dreamt possible.

The Desire For The Quick Fix

You may have realised that I'm a bit of a fan of horsemanship and taking a more thoughtful and empathetic approach to horse training.

And this is where I risk being slightly controversial, but I will try and explain my thoughts as diplomatically as possible.

Often when riders have issues with their horses under saddle, they start looking for answers in the form of quick fixes, magic supplements or extra equipment. If a horse pulls on the reins, it might be instinctive to start wondering whether the bit you are using is the problem. If a horse throws his head up, maybe a martingale might fix it. Or 'my horse is being a bit nutty and high strung – perhaps a calming supplement will help'.

Now in certain circumstances, all these things could be perfectly valid. Martingales, alternative bits, and calming supplements all have their place for the right reasons (calcium/magnesium deficiencies or imbalance, Vitamin B deficiencies, horse is more comfortable in a different style of bit etc.!).

But I do want to draw your attention to the fact that whilst it's instinctive for us as humans to want to find a quick fix to our problems with our horses, often it comes down to training and not the equipment.

And this is coming from someone who owns a saddlery! Because even when a rider comes in to my store asking about bigger bits and martingales etc, I will go to great pains to try and understand the real root issue and make a very honest judgement call to the best of my abilities as to whether that particular piece of equipment is likely to be of assistance. And yep – even when it means we lose a sale!

For me, if a horse is really anxious and therefore throws his head up too high for example (which is very common!), then it's best to try and help the horse to let go of that anxiety, rather than trying to prevent him from lifting his head (which he feels he needs to do) with a martingale – which much of the time will simply make the anxiety worse (as you're essentially stopping him from expressing himself and forcing him into behaving).

But I say all this in the most loving and understanding way – simply as food for thought.

If in Doubt – Get Help!

My final word of advice is that if you find yourself struggling to fix a problem or issue with your horse or are simply doubting your own abilities or whether you are doing anything right or not – is to simply try and bring in some expert help.

Now ultimately your best option here is to employ the services of a professional horse trainer or possibly a riding instructor who can physically be there with you to guide you. You may be able to get someone to come to you – or you may need to float your horse to another facility. A private lesson even occasionally can be really helpful.

If you are restricted by budget, sometimes it's also really great to attend a group clinic locally. This can often be cheaper as the cost of a trainers time is split between participants and it also allows you to get your horse out to somewhere different, meet new people and watch others with their horses.

If you are in Australia and would like to understand horsemanship and training better, I highly recommend Justin Colquhoun from Elite Horsemanship, as he has a brilliant teaching style that is supportive and encouraging. He appears in many areas across the country (and has started going internationally too!) so look him up and see if he might suit you. He completely transformed my relationship with my young horse over the course of a two day clinic.

These days though location is no longer such an inhibitor when it comes to accessing information. If you are at a point where you need help but cannot bring an instructor in or attend a clinic – the internet is now your best friend.

Many big name trainers and coaches offer online programs that you can study at your own pace. You simply watch their training videos and then apply it to your own horse. Obviously this has it's limitations in that your horse may do something slightly differently to the horses shown on the videos etc. But if you are desperate for some basics it's a good place to start.

My favourite person in my own journey with my young Thoroughbred has been Warwick Schiller. His online video subscription service offers a massive array of training videos that solve just about any problem that you may have. What's even more valuable – is the principles and approach to horses that he teaches.

Warwick has a massive YouTube Channel that you can find with plenty of free and very useful and insightful content.

I'd also highly recommend looking in to Ross Jacobs at Good Horsemanship. Both his books and blog posts are well worth reading.

But it doesn't matter who you choose as such. Do some hunting around, ask around, do a Google search or Facebook search – and see who resonates with you.

The details for the above-mentioned names are also included in the 'Resources' section at the end of this book.

CHAPTER 12:
Putting it all together!

Woweee! You've made it to the very last chapter, wahoooo! And now that you have come this far, it's time to put everything together, wrap things up and point you in the direction of more detailed assistance.

We've covered a fair bit of ground throughout this book, from the practical aspects of getting stuff done with horses with your kids attached, right through to mindset strategies, conquering fear and some basics around horse training.

It's my hope that the processes and tips in this book can put you on a more inspired and successful path which will allow you to make the kid-horse juggling act much, much easier.

At the very least, I hope I have provided you with the encouragement that combining horses and motherhood is really truly possible – and whilst a challenge at times – incredibly rewarding and IMPORTANT.

Please know if there is one single thing I can achieve with this book – is for you to know that it is OK as a mum to still keep your own dreams and passions firmly in place. And that you don't need to feel guilty or selfish for wanting to keep a piece of you.

Allowing yourself - and demanding some time out from kids and family life - to do something that you love to do is absolutely VITAL to your own health and sanity.

You will be a better, happier and healthier mum WITH horses.

That I can promise!

It's a matter of taking these strategies and finding ways to make it all work for you. Trust that gut instinct and motherly instinct of yours!

Sarah Walkerden

Experiment and have fun!

But as with any book, there is always a limit on exactly how much you can really include between these humble pages.

And realistically you will most likely need some hands on help, guidance and support in order to achieve your horse riding goals alongside raising healthy and happy children.

So this is where we have put together a brief list of useful resources that I myself have personally used and what's worked for other Horsey Mums. These are mindset coaches, horse trainers and the like who might just be useful to you too.

You've already been introduced to a few names but the full details are in the Resources section to follow.

There is also another little initiative I'd love to mention, just in case you feel the need to join a community of other 'Horsey Mums' if the support is lacking around you.

It's become ever so clear to me over the past year or two that us 'Horsey Mums' face such unique challenges and are very unique individuals. And there just isn't any real specific support catering just for us.

Therefore, I'm very proud to introduce you to the Horsey Mums Collective. Here, we are creating a safe, supportive community of 'Horsey Mums' where you can get access to stacks of great learning content (that takes all the learnings in this book to a much deeper level!), and also provides exclusive access to a Facebook community full of 'Horsey Mums' who are just like you.

To help get you started, our FREE Five Day Email Challenge is awesome, which you can access here: http://bit.ly/2QnxSGr.

As an extra bonus for my fabulous book-readers, we also have a special offer where you can join our Membership with your first month absolutely FREE!

Your FREEBIE Coupon Code is: **GYX9RBCN95**.

We hope to see you within our community soon!

But it's time to wrap this up and for you to stop reading, so you can start implementing these ideas and get back on that horse pronto!

Hop to it – make a start – and good luck!

Sarah xoxoxoxox

Resources

For further information, please peruse this list of helpful experts who can continue to help in any area you desire as a 'Horsey Mum'.

Please note I have no affiliation for any of the people recommended here. They have not paid for any mention in this book, they are simply who I have found to be useful.

Mindset, Fear & Goal Setting

Jane Pike
Confident Rider
Web: http://www.confidentrider.club

Natasha Altoff-Kelly
The Riding Success Institute
Web: http://www.theridingsuccessinstitute.com

Tanja Mitton
Equestrian Success & Mindset
Web: https://www.tanjamitton.com

Horse Trainers

Warwick Schiller
Web: https://www.warwickschiller.com
YouTube: https://www.youtube.com/user/WarwickSchiller

Ross Jacobs
Web: http://www.goodhorsemanship.com.au
YouTube:
https://www.youtube.com/channel/UCPMhpvRw8CHYelTy8wL12IA

Justin Colquhoun
Web: https://elitehorsemanship.com

Horsey Mums

More handy FREE resources can be found at
https://horseymumscollective.com/project/freebies/

Or you can join our FREE Five Day Email Challenge here:
http://bit.ly/2QnxSGr.

About The Author

Sarah is Owner/Manager of One Stop Horse Shop (alongside husband Toby), which includes a large online store selling all sorts of quality, affordable horse gear – and a full-time physical retail store in country Victoria, in Smythesdale, which is 10 minutes out of Ballarat.

One Stop Horse Shop, under Sarah's leadership, has one simple mission – to make as many horse riding dreams come true for as many riders as possible – with high quality and very affordable gear.

With two young children – Oliver (6) and Sophie (3) she knows full well how challenging it can be to juggle kids, family, work and LIFE with horses! But she has also experienced the benefits of doing so.

Her own personal mission is to empower as many 'Horsey Mums' as possible to continue pursuing their dreams after kids with the Horsey Mums Collective.

Sarah, Toby and the kids live in Berringa, on 70 acres, 40km South West of Ballarat, with 3 horses and 6 crazy chickens!

Her current two horses, Jack (retired Standardbred) and her main beau 'Trigger' (the very unsuccessful ex-racing Thoroughbred!) keep her happy, entertained and somewhat sane in the craziness of life, business and kids.

The kids own 'Snowball' a little black & shaggy Shetland/Miniature pony, who thoroughly enjoys stirring up trouble with Sarah's big horses.

In another previous life, Sarah spent 13 years in the 'Corporate World' working as a Web Content Specialist. Besides horses, writing is another great love!

Sarah Walkerden

Acknowledgements

One simply cannot publish a book, without offering a few final words of thanks, to my nearest and dearest...

Toby Billing – My (somewhat) charming husband! Who is ultimately my bestest friend.

Oliver & Sophie Billing – My beautiful children, who drive me to the brink of insanity and back, but who I wouldn't change for the world.

Robert & Jenni Walkerden – My incredible non-horsey parents, who have suffered through many cold horse events, trudged through muddy paddocks in the dark, poo picked paddocks, and have always been there to support my crazy dreams.

Cameron Walkerden – My ambitious older brother who has always taught and inspired me to aim higher!

Peter Walkerden – My cruisy little brother who has always reminded me to chill the hell out!

Lynne & Noel Billing – My amazingly supportive in-laws, who I simply adore.

Leanne Leighton – For being an amazing employee, friend and my right-hand woman!

Rebecca, Jade, Denise, Trish, Amy & Caroline – My amazing 'Mummies Group' and best friends – so glad our babies bought us together!

And to all other friends, family, mentors and associates – I thank you!

Sarah Walkerden

For More Information:

Website:
www.onestophorse.com.au

Address:
27 Brooke Street
Smythesdale VIC 3351

Phone:
03 4301 7383

Website:
www.horseymumscollective.com

Phone:
03 4301 7383

Sarah Walkerden

BONUS GOAL SETTING WORKSHEET

Welcome to your very own Horsey Mums Goal Setting Worksheet!

Once you've finished reading this book, you might like to fill this out. It will allow you to figure out (and write down!) what it is you'd ideally like your life and horsey dreams to look like and then determine some basic steps as to how you can work towards achieving these goals.

My Ultimate Dream With My Horse is...

_____

_____

_____

The Steps I Need To Take To Get There...

1.	6.
2.	7.
3.	8.
4.	9.
5.	10.

My 12 Month Target is...

_____

_____

My 12 Month Plan is...

Month	Goal To Achieve	Month	Goal To Achieve
1.		7.	
2.		8.	
3.		9.	
4.		10.	
5.		11.	
6.		12.	

My Ideal Daily & Weekly Schedule Would Look Like...

Monday:

Morning	Afternoon

Tuesday:

Morning	Afternoon

Wednesday:

Morning	Afternoon

Thursday:

Morning	Afternoon

Friday:

Morning	Afternoon

Sarah Walkerden

Saturday:

Morning	Afternoon

Sunday:

Morning	Afternoon

NOTES

_____

_____

_____

_____

_____

_____

_____

_____

_____

_____

_____

_____

_____

_____

_____

_____

_____

_____

_____

_____

_____

_____

Sarah Walkerden